Moonhee L. Cho's Vol.2 " Korean Study by Moonhee C." CONTENTS

Copyright© 2014 USA Libruary of Congress Txu 1-923-755,   ISBN 978-1540-796073

No.1 **Korean Letter Shapes** (한글의 구조) P.1

No.2 King SeZong and his Status photo (세종대왕과 그의 동상사진) P.2-3

No.3 Korean Alphabet (한국어의 자음과 모음) P.4-7

No.4 Korean Alphabet Chart by Moonhee L. Cho [조(이) 문희 } P. 8

No.5   Moon, Crickets Songs Introductions (달, 귀뚜리 노래) P.9-10

No.6 Brushing Teeth Song (이를 닦자 노래) P. 11-12

No.7 School Bell Song (학교종 노래) P.13-14

No.8 Korean National Flag and Anthem (태극기 노래와 애국가) P.15-19

No.9 Sam Yil Zuhl Song Introduction (삼일절 노래) P.20-22

No.10 DongNe BangNe Song (동네 방네 소문났네 노래) P. 23-24

No.11 Greetings and Introduction (인사와 소개) P. 25-26

No.12 Korean Letters and BadChim (한글과 받침) P. 27-29

No.13 Korean Basic Sentence's Pattern (한글의 기본 문장형식) P.30-32

No.14 Hangeul's Classifications (한글의 품사구분) P.33-48

No.15   The Family Relations (가족관계) P.49-53

No.16 The Korean Proverbs (한국 속담집) P.54-63

No.17 The Mimesis and Onomatopoeia (의태어와 의성어) P.64-82

No. 18 Korean Simple Vocaburary Lists (간단한 한글 단어집) P.83-113

No.19 My Dreans are where I am (나의 꿈은 내가 있는 곳에) P.114

i

No.1 Korean letter Shapes (한글의 구조)

한글의 구조는 두 가지이다.

Pronunciation (**sounds like**) (han-geul-euy gu-zo-neun do ga-zi-i-da)

Translation ;   Korean letters have two shapes.

Shape 1.----   자음 (Consonant) + 모음 (Vowel)

Shape 2. ----   자음 (Consonant) + 모음 (Vowel) + 받침 (Badchim)

ex.   한국어 공부 (HanGugUh GongBu)

한 -- ㅎ (a consonant) + ㅏ (a vowel) + ㄴ (a BadChim)

Sounds like (Han)   H   a   n

국 -- ㄱ (a consonant) + ㅜ (a vowel) + ㄱ (a BadChim)

Sounds   like (Gug)   G   u   g

어 --   ㅇ (a consonant) + ㅓ (a vowel)

Sounds   like (uh=ouh)   O   uh

공 -- ㄱ (a consonant) + ㅗ (a vowel) + ㅇ (a BadChim)

Sounds   like (Gong)   G   o   ng

부 -- ㅂ (a consonant) + ㅜ (a vowel)

Sounds   like (Bu)   B   u

No. 2 King SeZong and photo of his Status (세종대왕과 그의 동상사진)

세종대왕께서 한국말을 한글로 서기 1443년에 창조하셨습니다.

(se-zong-dae-wang-gge-suh han-gug-mal-eul han-geul-ro

suh-gi 1443 (chun sa-baeg-sa-sib-sam) nyhn-e chang-zo ha-syuhtss-seum-ni-da)

@ The King SeZong created the Korean Letters in AD 1443 from the Korean language.

세종대왕께서 창조하신 글자 즉 훈민정음이 한글입니다.

se-zong-dae-wang-gge-suh chang-zo-ha-sin geul-za zeug,

hun-min-zuhng-eum-i han-geul-im-ni-da

@ The Hun-Min-Zuhng-Eum which is King SeZong created has been called the HanGeul.

한글은 자음 14 자와 모음 21 자로 구성 되었습니다.

han-geul-eun za-eum 14 (yuhl-ne)-za-wa mo-eum

21 (seu-mul-han) za-ro gu-suhng-dwoe-uhtss-seum-ni-da

@ The Korean letters consist of 14 consonants and 21 vowels.

단어 (Vocabuarly)

세종 (a name of king) 대왕 (King)

께서 (a subjective suffix , a honoring shape of " 이 ") 한국 (Korea)

말 (language) 을 (a objective suffix = o.s.) 한글 (Korean letter) 로 (to)

서기 (AD) 년 (year) 에 (in) 창조하셨습니다 (honoring word of 창조하다 (create)

글자 (글) (letters) 즉 (that is) 구성 (consist of)

훈민정음 (the original letters that King SeZong created) 자음 (consonant) 모음 (vowel)

No.3 Korean Alphabet (한글의 자음과 모음)

The pronuciations has illustrated by Moonhee L. Cho [조(이) 문희]

@ 14 자음 (Za Eum ; Consonants) 과 21 모음 (Mo Eum ; Vowels)

@ 14 자음

ㄱ (Gi Yuhg) ㄴ (Ni Eun) ㄷ (Di Geud) ㄹ (Ri Eul) ㅁ (Mi Eum)

ㅂ (Bi Eub) ㅅ (Si Ots) ㅇ (Yi Eung) ㅈ (Zi Eutz) ㅊ (Chi Eut)

ㅋ (Ki Yuhg) ㅌ (Ti Geut) ㅍ (Pi Eup) ㅎ (Hi Eut)

@ 21 모음

ㅏ (a) ㅑ (ya) ㅓ (eo , uh) ㅕ (yuh) ㅗ (o) ㅛ (yo) ㅜ (u) ㅠ (yu)

ㅡ (eu) ㅣ (i) ㅐ (ae) ㅒ (yae) ㅔ (e) ㅖ (ye) ㅘ (wa)

ㅙ (wae) ㅚ (woe) ㅝ (wou) ㅞ (weh) ㅟ (wi) ㅢ (euh) or (euy) or (ee)

@ 한글판 (han-geul-pan Korean Alphabet)

ㄱ (Gi Yuhg, G sound)

가 (Ga) 갸 (Gya) 거 (Guh) 겨 (Gyuh) 고 (Go) 교 (Gyo) 구 (Gu) 규 (Gyu)

그 (Geu) 기 (Gi) 개 (Gae) 걔 (Gyae) 게 (Ge) 계 (Gye) 과 (Gwa)

괘 (Gwae) 괴 (Gwoe) 궈 (Gwou) 궤 (Gweh) 귀 (Gwi) 긔 (Geuy)

ㄴ (Ni Eun, N sound)

나 (Na) 냐 (Nya) 너 (Nuh) 녀 (Nyuh) 노 (No) 뇨 (Nyo) 누 (Nu) 뉴 (Nyu)

느 (Neu) 니 (Ni) 내 (Nae) 냬 (Nyae) 네 (Ne) 녜 (Nye) 놔 (Nwa)

놰 (Nwae) 뇌 (Nwoe) 눠 (Nwou) 눼 (Nweh) 뉘 (Nwi) 늬 (Neuy)

ㄷ (Di Geud, D sound)

다 (Da) 댜 (Dya) 더 (Duh) 뎌 (Dyuh) 도 (Do) 됴 (Dyo) 두 (Du) 듀 (Dyu)

드 (Deu) 디(Di) 대 (Dae) 대 (Dyae) 데 (De) 뎨 (Dye) 돠 (Dwa)

돼 (Dwae) 되 (Dwoe) 둬 (Dwou) 뒈 (Dweh) 뒤 (Dwi) 듸 (Deuy)

ㄹ (Ri Eul, R sound)

라 (Ra) 랴(Rya) 러 (Ruh) 려 (Ryuh) 로 (Ro) 료 (Ryo) 루 (Ru) 류 (Ryu)

르 (Reu) 리 (Ri) 래 (Rae) 럐 (Ryae) 레 (Re) 례 (Rye) 롸 (Rwa)

뢔 (Rwae) 뢰 (Rwoe) 뤄 (Rwou) 뤠 (Rweh) 뤼 (Rwi) 릐 (Reuy)

ㅁ (Mi Eum, M sound)

마 (Ma) 먀 (Mya) 머(Muh) 며(Myuh) 모(Mo)묘(Myo) 무 (Mu) 뮤 (Myu)

므 (Meu) 미 (Mi) 매 (Mae) 먜 (Myae) 메 (Me) 몌 (Mye) 뫄 (Mwa)

뫠 (Mwae) 뫼 (Mwoe) 뭐 (Mwou) 뭬 (Mweh) 뮈(Mwi) 믜 (Meuy)

ㅂ (Bi Eub, B sound)

바 (Ba) 뱌 (Bya) 버 (Buh) 벼 (Byuh) 보 (Bo) 뵤 (Byo) 부 (Bu) 뷰 (Byu)

브 (Beu) 비(Bi) 배 (Bae) 뱨 (Byae) 베 (Be) 볘 (Bye) 봐 (Bwa)

봬 (Bwae) 뵈 (Bwoe) 붜 (Bwou) 붸 (Bweh) 뷔 (Bwi) 븨 (Beuy)

ㅅ (Si ots,   S sound)

사 (Sa) 샤 (Sya) 서 (Suh) 셔 (Syuh) 소 (So) 쇼 (Syo) 수 (Su) 슈(Syu)

스 (Seu) 시 (Si) 새 (Sae) 섀 (Syae) 세 (Se) 셰 (Sye) 솨 (Swa)

쇄 (Swae) 쇠 (Swoe) 숴 (Swou) 쉐 (Sweh) 쉬 (Swi) 싀(Seuy)

ㅇ (Yi Eung, Yi sound or ommnited and ng sounds)

아 (a) 야 (ya) 어 (uh) 여 (yuh) 오 (o) 요 (yo) 우(u) 유 (yu)

으 (eu) 이 (i) 애 (ae) 얘 (yae) 에 (e) 예 (ye) 와 (wa)

왜 (wae) 외 (woe) 워 (wou) 웨 (weh) 위 (wi) 의 (euh) or (euy) or (ee)

ㅈ (Zi Eutz   Z sound)

자 (Za) 쟈 (Zya) 저 (Zuh) 져 (Zyuh) 조 (Zo) 죠 (Zyo) 주 (Zu) 쥬 (Zyu)

즈 (Zeu) 지 (Zi) 재 (Zae) 쟤 (Zyae) 제 (Ze) 졔 (Zye) 좌 (Zwa)

좨 (Zwae) 죄 (Zwoe) 줘 (Zwou) 줴 (Zweh) 쥐 (Zwi) 즤 (Zeuy)

ㅊ (Chi Euts Ch sound)

차 (Cha) 챠 (Chya) 처 (Chuh) 쳐 (Chyuh) 초 (Cho) 쵸 (Chyo) 추 (Chu) 츄 (Chyu)

츠 (Cheu) 치 (Chi) 채 (Chae) 챼 (Chyae) 체 (Che) 쳬 (Chye) 촤 (Chwa)

쵀 (Chwae) 최 (Chwoe) 춰 (Chwou) 췌 (Chweh) 취 (Chwi) 츼 (Chee)

ㅋ (Ki Yuhk, K sound),

카 (Ka) 캬 (Kya) 커 (Kuh) 켜 (Kyuh) 코 (Ko) 쿄 (Kyo) 쿠 (Ku) 큐 (Kyu)

크 (Keu) 키 (Ki) 캐 (Kae) 컈 (Kyae) 케 (Ke) 켸 (Kye) 콰 (Kwa)

쾌 (Kwae) 쾨 (kwoe) 쿼 (Kou) 퀘 (Kweh) 퀴 (Kwi) 킈 (Kee)

ㅌ (Ti Geut   T sound)

타 (Ta) 탸 (Tya) 터 (Tuh) 텨 (Tyuh) 토 (To) 툐 (Tyo) 투 (Tu) 튜 (Tyu)

트 (Teu) 티 (Ti) 태 (Tae) 턔 (Tyae) 테 (Te) 톄 (Tye) 톼 (Twa)

퇘 (Twae) 퇴 (Twoe) 퉈 (Tou) 퉤 (Tweh) 튀 (Twi) 틔 (Tee)

ㅍ (Pi Eup,   P sound)

파 (Pa) 퍄 (Pya) 퍼 (Puh) 펴 (Pyuh) 포 (Po) 표 (Pyo) 푸 (Pu) 퓨 (Pyu)

프 (Peu) 피 (Pi) 패 (Pae) 퍠 (Pyae) 페 (Pe) 폐 (Pye) 퐈 (Pwa)

퐤 (Pwae) 푀 (Pwoe) 풔 (Pou) 풰 (Pweh) 퓌 (Pwi) 픠 (Peuy)

ㅎ (Hi Euth, H sound)

하 (Ha) 햐 (Hya) 허 (Huh) 혀 (Hyuh) 호 (Ho) 효 (Hyo) 후 (Hu) 휴 (Hyu)

흐 (Heu) 히 (Hi) 해 (Hae) 해 (Hyae) 헤 (He) 혜 (Hye) 화(Hwa)

왜 (Hwae) 회 (Hwoe) 훠 (Hou) 웨 (Hweh) 휘 (Hwi) 희 (Hee)

@ 이중자음 (yi-zung za-eum   Double Consonants)

1. 쌍자음 (ssang-za-eum Twin Consonants)

ㄲ (Ssang Gi Yuhg   G,K,H   mixed sounds , marked with gg)

ㄸ (Ssang Di Geud   D,T,H mixed sounds, marked with dd)

ㅃ (Ssang Bi Eub   B,P,H mixed sounds, marked with bb)

ㅉ (Ssang Zi Euz   Z,T,S mixed sounds marked with zz   )

ㅆ (Ssang Si Ots   S,T,H mixed sounds, marked with ss)

2 혼합자음 (hon-hab-za-eum   Mixed Consonant)

ㄳ, ㄵ, ㄶ, ㅄ, ㄺ,   ㄻ ㄼ ㄽ ㄾ ㄿ ㅀ

혼합자음은 받침에만 쓰인다 (hon-hab-za-eum-eun bad-chim-e-man sseu-in-da)

The mixed consonants are only used in the BadChim.

\# More details about the BadChim (받침) on chapter 12.

@ 이 한글판의 어떤 글자들은 한글단어에 쓰인 적이 없으나 외래어를 표기하는데 쓰였습니다

yi han-geul-pan-euy uh-dduhn geul-za-deul-eun han-geul-dan-uh-e

sseu-in zuhg-i uhbs-eu-na woe-rae-uh-reul pyo=gi-ha-neun-de sseu-yuhss-seum-ni-da

p.s.   Some letters in this chart had never been used to Korean words

but had used for describes the foreign languages.

한글판 (Han-geul's Alphabets & Sounds chart)
by Moonhee L'cho (조 문희) 2014

14 Consonants (자음) / 21 Vowels (모음)	ㅏ a	ㅑ ya	ㅓ uh/yuh	ㅕ yuh	ㅗ o/yo	ㅛ yo	ㅜ u	ㅠ yu	ㅡ eu	ㅣ i	ㅐ ae/yae	ㅒ yae	ㅔ e/ye	ㅖ ye	ㅘ wa	ㅙ wae	ㅚ woe	ㅝ wou	ㅞ weh	ㅟ wi	ㅢ euh/euy
ㄱ G g:yuh	가 ga	갸 gya	거 guh	겨 gyuh	고 go	교 gyo	구 gu	규 gyu	그 geu	기 gi	개 gae	걔 gyae	게 ge	계 gye	과 gwa	괘 gwae	괴 gwoe	궈 gwou	궤 gweh	귀 gwi	긔 guy/gee
ㄴ N n:eun	나 na	냐 nya	너 nuh	녀 nyuh	노 no	뇨 nyo	누 nu	뉴 nyu	느 neuh	니 ni	내 nae	냬 nyae	네 ne	녜 nye	놔 nwa	놰 nwae	뇌 nwoe	눠 nwou	눼 nweh	뉘 nwi	늬 ndy/nee
ㄷ D d:geut	다 da	댜 dya	더 duh	뎌 dyuh	도 do	됴 dyo	두 du	듀 dyu	드 deuh	디 di	대 dae	댸 dyae	데 de	뎨 dye	돠 dwa	돼 dwae	되 dwoe	둬 dwou	뒈 tweh	뒤 dwi	듸 day/dee
ㄹ R r:eul	라 ra	랴 rya	러 ruh	려 ryuh	로 ro	료 ryo	루 ru	류 ryu	르 reuh	리 r'i	래 rae	럐 ryae	레 re	례 rye	롸 rwa	뢔 rwae	뢰 rwoe	뤄 rwou	뤠 rweh	뤼 rwi	릐 vay/ree
ㅁ M m:eum	마 ma	먀 mya	머 muh	며 myuh	모 mo	묘 myo	무 mu	뮤 myu	므 meuh	미 m'i	매 mae	먜 myae	메 me	몌 mye	뫄 mwa	뫠 mwae	뫼 mwoe	뭐 mwou	뭬 mweh	뮈 mwi	믜 may/mee
ㅂ B b:eub	바 ba	뱌 bya	버 buh	벼 byuh	보 bo	뵤 byo	부 bu	뷰 byu	브 beuh	비 b'i	배 bae	뱨 byae	베 be	볘 bye	봐 bwa	봬 bwae	뵈 bwoe	붜 bwou	붸 bweh	뷔 bwi	븨 bay/bee
ㅅ S s:eus	사 sa	샤 sya	서 suh	셔 syuh	소 so	쇼 syo	수 su	슈 syu	스 seuh	시 s'i	새 sae	섀 syae	세 se	셰 sye	솨 swa	쇄 swae	쇠 swoe	숴 swou	쉐 sweh	쉬 swi	싀 say/see
ㅇ Ng (at Batchim) ng/y:eung	아 a	야 ya	어 uh	여 yuh	오 o/yo	요 yo	우 u	유 yu	으 eu	이 i	애 ae	얘 yae	에 e	예 ye	와 wa	왜 wae	외 woe	워 wou	웨 weh	위 wi	의 ey/ee
ㅈ Z z:eut	자 za	쟈 zya	저 zuh	져 zyuh	조 zo	죠 zyo	주 zu	쥬 zyu	즈 zeuh	지 z'i	재 zae	쟤 zyae	제 ze	졔 zye	좌 zwa	좨 zwae	죄 zwoe	줘 zwou	줴 zweh	쥐 zwi	즤 zuy/zee
ㅊ Ch ch:eut	차 cha	챠 chya	처 chuh	쳐 chyuh	초 cho	쵸 chyo	추 chu	츄 chyu	츠 cheuh	치 ch'i	채 chae	챼 chyae	체 che	쳬 chye	촤 chwa	쵀 chwae	최 chwoe	춰 chwou	췌 chweh	취 chwi	츼 chuy/chee
ㅋ K k:yuk	카 ka	캬 kya	커 kuh	켜 kyuh	코 ko	쿄 kyo	쿠 ku	큐 kyu	크 keuh	키 k'i	캐 kae	컈 kyae	케 ke	켸 kye	콰 kwa	쾌 kwae	쾨 kwoe	쿼 kwou	퀘 kweh	퀴 kwi	킈 kuy/kee
ㅌ T t:eut	타 ta	탸 tya	터 tuh	텨 tyuh	토 to	툐 tyo	투 tu	튜 tyu	트 teuh	티 t'i	태 tae	턔 tyae	테 te	톄 tye	톼 twa	퇘 twae	퇴 twoe	퉈 twou	퉤 tweh	튀 twi	틔 tuy/tee
ㅍ P p:eup	파 pa	퍄 pya	퍼 puh	펴 pyuh	포 po	표 pyo	푸 pu	퓨 pyu	프 peuh	피 p'i	패 pae	퍠 pyae	페 pe	폐 pye	퐈 pwa	퐤 pwae	푀 pwoe	풔 pwou	풰 pweh	퓌 pwi	픠 puy/pee
ㅎ H h:eut	하 ha	햐 hya	허 huh	혀 hyuh	호 ho	효 hyo	후 hu	휴 hyu	흐 heu	히 h'i	해 hae	햬 hyae	헤 he	혜 hye	화 hwa	홰 hwae	회 hwoe	훠 hwou	훼 hweh	휘 hwi	희 huy/hee

14 Consonents

※ Some letters in this chart never been used for Korean words but describes the foreign languages.
(이 한글판 모음에 몇개 글자들은 한번도 한국말에 사용된적이 없으며, 외래어 표기에만 쓰인다.)

No.5 The Moon ,Crickets Songs Introductions (달,귀뚜리 노래 소개)

@ 달 노래 (The Moon Song)

달 달 무슨 달   Moon moon what kind of moon

dal dal mu-seun dal

쟁반 같이 둥근 달 Round moon like a dish

zaeng-ban-gat-i dung-geun dal

어디 어디 떴나   Where has it rizen ?

uh-di uh-di dduhts-na

남산 위에 떴지   Risen over the NamSan

nam-sa-wi-e dduhts-zi

단어 (Vocabulary)

달 (moon) 무슨 (what kind of) 쟁반 (dish) 같이 (as like) 둥근 (round) 어디 (where) 떴나 (risen ?) 남산 (a mountain's name in Seoul) 위에 (over) 떴지 (has risen)

@ 귀뚜라미 노래 (The Crickets Song)

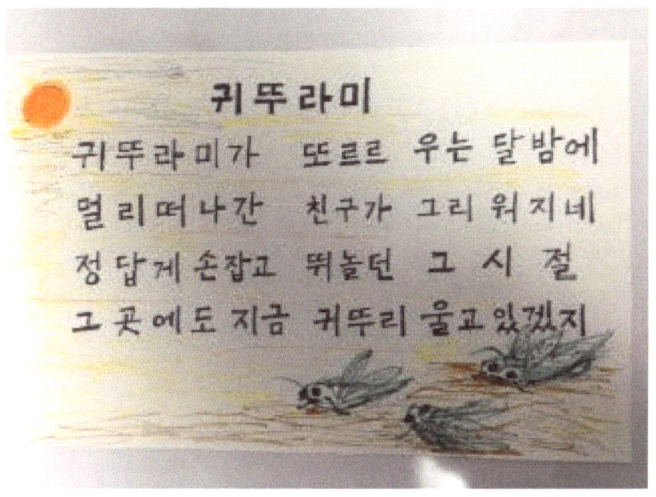

귀뚜라미가 또르르 우는 달밤에 gwi-ddu-ra-mi-ga ddo-reu-reu wu-neun dal-bam-e

The moonlight over the crickets ddo-reu-reu cring

멀리 떠나간 친구가 그리워지네 muhl-ri dduh-na-gan chin-gu-ga geu-ri-wou-zi-ne

longing for a friend left   faraway

정답게 손잡고 뛰놀던 그 시절 zung-dap-ge son-zab-go ddwi-nol-duhn geu si-zuhl

The time we played together, holding   hands

그 곳에도 지금 귀뚜리 울고 있겠지 geu gots-e-do zi-geum gwi-ddu-ri wul-go-itss-getss-zi

Guessing that the crickets would cring over there too

단어 (Vocabulary)

귀뚜라미 (cricket) 가 (s.s.) 또르르 (a onomotopoeia) 우는(cring)달 (moon)밤 (night) 에 (at, in) 멀리 (far) 떠나간 (gone) 친구(friend)가 (objective.s) 그리워지네 (longing for) 정답게 (friendly) 손 (hand) 잡고 (holding)뛰 (jump) 놀던 (played) 그 (that) 시절(time)그곳 (there) 에 (at) 도(too) 지금 (now) 울고 (cry) 있겠지(may be, guess)

No.6 Brushing Teeth Song (이를 닦자 노래)

이를 닦자 깨끗이 Brushing teeth clean

Yi-reul Dagg-za Ggae-Ggeus-i

아침 일찍 일어나 Get up early in the morning

Ah-chim Yil-zzig Yil-uh-na

이 방긋 나 방긋 Teeth bang-geut I bang-geut

YI Bang-geut Na Bang-geut

너 방긋 나 방긋 You bang-geut I bang-geut

Nuh Bang-geut Na Bang-geut

웃는 이는 하얀이 Smiley teeth are white teeth

Wut-neun-yi-neun Ha-yan-yi

성난 이는 누런이 Angry teeth are yellow teeth

Sung-nan-yi-neun Nu-ruhn-yi

이 방긋 나 방긋 Teeth bang-geut I bang-geut

YI Bang-geut Na Bang-geut

너 방긋 나 방긋 You bang-geut I bang-geut

Nuh Bang-geut Na Bang-geut

단어 (Vocabulary)

이 (teeth) 닦자 (brushing or polishing) 깨끗이(cleanly)

...를 (a objective suffix after the word that has no batdchim ,받침)

예, # 나는 사과를 먹는다. I am eating an apple

당신은 노래를 부른다   you are singing.

그는 기타를 친다   He is playing the guitar.

나 (na ,I) 는 (neun a sujecting suffix) 사과 (sa-gwa apple)

먹는다 (mug-neun-da ,eat) 당신 (dang-sin you) 노래 (no-rae ,song)

부른다 (bu-reun-da sing)그는 (geu-neun, he, s.s) 기타 (gi-ta ,guitar) 친다 (chin-da, play)

...을 (a objective suffix after the word that has yes batdchim)

예, # 그녀는 밥을 먹는다 She is eating the Bab.

학생은 펜을 좋아한다 The students likes the pen.

나는 여행을 간다 I am going on trip.

그녀 (geu-nyuh she) 밥 (bab, rice) 학생 (hag-saeng ,student)

펜 (pen, pen is the foreign language) 좋아한다 (zoh-a-han-da like)

여행 (yuh-haeng, trip) 간다 (gan-da,go) 아침 (morning) 일찍 (early)

일어나 (다) (get up) 방긋 (a mimesis word for shape of smile)

웃는 (다) (smile) 성난(angry)

No.7 school Bell Song (학교종 노래)

아기가 자라서 학교에 갑니다   Ah-gi-ga Za-ra-suh Hag-gyo-e Gamb-ni-da

Baby is growing up and going to school

학교에는 선생님이 계시고   Hag-gyo-eh-neun Suhn-saeng-nim-yi Gyeh-si-go

Teachers are at the school

학생들이 모입니다   Hag-saeng-deul-i Mo-imb-ni-da

Students are gathering

학교종 소리를 들으며 Hag-gyo-zong So-ri-reul Deul-eu-myuh

Hear the school bell's ring

공부하러 갑니다   Gong-bu-ha-ruh Gamb-ni-da

Going to study

노래도 배웁니다   No-rae-do Bae-wumb-ni-da

and learn songs

@   학교종 노래   (Song)

\# 학교종이 땡땡땡 Hag-gyo-zong-i Ddang-ddang-ddang

School bell rings ddaeng-ddaeng-ddaeng

\# 어서 모이자   Uh-suh Mo-i-za

Hurry get together

\# 선생님이 우리를 기다리신다   Suhn-saeng-nim-i Wu-ri-reul Gi-da-ri-sin-da

Teacher is waiting for us.

단어 (Vocabulary)

아기 (baby) 자라서 (grow up)학교(school) 선생님(teacher)학생(student)

모이다 (gether) 종 (bell) 소리 (sound)땡땡땡 (a Onomotopoeia for bell rings)

들으며 (with listening) 공부 (study) ....하러 (for or to) 갑니다(go)어서 (hurry)

우리 (us) 를 (a objective suffix) 기다리다 (waiting)

신 for honoring particle 기다리신다 (waiting) 노래 (song) 배운다 (learning)

No.8 Korea's Natinal Flag and Anthem (태극기와 애국가)

태극기는 한국의 깃발 입니다.

Tae-geug-gi-neun Han-gug-euh Git-bal-imb-ni-da

Tae-Geug-Gi is Korea's National flag.

태극기 안에는 한국의 정신이 살고 있습니다.

Tae-geug-gi An-eh-neun Han-gug-euh Zuhng-sin-yi Sal-go-yitss-eum-ni-da

The Korean sprits live inside Tae-Geug-Gi

태극기의 그림 마다 뜻이 있습니다

Tae-geug-gi-euh Geu-rim Ma-da Ddeuts-i Yits-eum-ni-da.

Every script of TaeGeugGi has meanings

.그 그림의 색갈은 하양, 빨강, 파랑 그리고 까망색 입니다

Geu geu-rim-euh Saeg-gal-eun Ha-yanhg ,Bbal-gang

Pa-rang Geu-ri-go Gg-mang-Saeg-imb-ni-da

The Script's colors are white, red, blue and black.

@　태극기 노래 (TaeGeugGi Song)

태극기가 바람에 펄럭입니다   Tae-geuk-gi-ga Ba-ram-eh Puhl-ruhk-yibm-ni-da

Taegeuggi is waving in the wind.

태극기는 우리나라 깃발입니다   Tae-geug-gi-neun Uh-ri-na-ra Gits-bal-yimb-ni-da

Taegeuggi is our country's flag.

단어 (Vocabulary)

깃발(flag) 안(inside) 정신(spirit) 살다(live)그림(picture) 의(possessive suffix)

마다 (every) 뜻 (meaning) 색 (color) 하양(white) 빨강 (red) 파랑 (blue)까망 (black)
바람 (wind) 에 (in) 펄럭이다 (wave)우리 (our)나라 (country) 깃발 (Flag)

@   애국가   (Korea's Natinal Anthem) (ae-gug-ga, no-rae)

.1.일절 (yil-zuhl, 1st words)

동해물과 백두산이 마르고 닳도록

dong-hae-mul-gwa baeg-du-san-i ma-reu-go dalrh-do-rog

Until east sea's water runs dry

하나님이 보우하사 우리나라 만세

ha-na-nim-i bo-u-ha-sa u-ri-na-ra-man-se

God protets our country for do Manse

후렴 (hu-ryum, refrain)

무궁화 삼천리 화려강산

mu-gung-hwa-sam-chun-ri hwa-ryh-gang-san

Mugung flowers are splendid over the rivers and mountains

대한사람 대한으로 길이 보존하세

dae-han-sa-ram dae-han-eu-ro gil-i-bo-zon-ha-se

The Koreans keep to Korea forever

2 이절 (yi-zuhl, 2nd words)

\# 남산위에 저소나무 철갑을 두른듯

nam-san-wi-e zuh-so-na-mu chuhl-gab-eul du-reun-deuts

Pine trees on Namsan look like an iron fence

\# 바람서리 불변함은 우리 기상일세

ba-ram-suh-ri bul-byuhn-ham-eun u-r gi-sang-il-sei

the winds and frosts are always our strengths

\# 무궁화 삼천리 화려강산

mu-gung-hwa sam-chuhn-ri hwa-ryuh-gang-san

Mugung flowers are   splendid over the rivers and mountains

\# 대한사람 대한으로 길이 보존하세

dae-han-sa-ram dae-han-eu-ro gil-i-bo-zon-ha-se

The Koreans keep to Korea forever

\# 후렴 (Refrain)

3.. 삼절 (sam-zuhl, 3rd words)

\# 가을하늘 공활한데 놓고 구름없이

ga-eul-ha-neul gong-hwal-han-de nop-go gu-reum-uhbs-i

Autumm's sky is high and clean without a cloud

\# 밝은 달은 우리가슴 일편단심일세

balg-eun dal-eun u-ri-ga-seum yil-pyuhn-dan-sim-il-se

The bright moon is our one heart always

\# 후렴 (Refrain)

\# 무궁화 삼천리 화려강산

\# 대한사람 대한으로 길이보존하세

4.. 사절 (sa-zuhl, 4th words)

\# 이 기상과 이 맘으로 충상을 다하여

yi-gi-sang-gwa yi mam-eu-ro chung-suhng-eul da-ha-yuh

This strength and mind have our full devotion

\# 괴로우나 즐거우나 나라 사랑하세

gwoe-ro-u-na zeul-guh-u-na na-ra sa-rang ha-se

Love our country in difficult or delight

\# 후렴 (Refrain)

\# 무궁화 삼천리 화려 강산

\# 대한사람 대한으로 길이보존하세

단어 (Vocabulary)

동해 (the East Sea) 물 (water) 과 (and) 백두산(BaegDu Mountain at very top of Korea)

이 (subjective suffix = s.s.) 마르 (v. 마르다 dry) 고 (and) 닳 (v. 닳다 worn out,)

도록 (until) 하나님 (God)이(s.s) 보우하사 (protect) 우리(our) 나라 (country)

만세 (a   celebrating gestures with two arms stretched up)

무궁화 (the symbol flower of Korea ; the rose of sharon)

삼천 (three thousand) 리 (a unit of distence, 1 리= about 0.3 mile)

화려 (splendor, brilliance) 강 (river) 산 (mountain) 대한 (Korea) 사람(people)

길이 (forever) 보존(keep, protect) 하세 (let's do)

남산 (Nam mountain which at center of Seoul) 위에 (above) 저 (that)

소나무 (pine tree) 철갑 (iron armor) 을 (a objective s)

두른 (v 두르다 fence, surounded) 듯 (looks) 바람 (wind)

서리(frost) 불반함 (never change) 은 (s.s)기상(strength) 일세 (is = 이다)

가을 (auttum) 하늘(sky) 공활(clean, empty) 한데 (thus)높고 (v 높다, high)

구름 (cloud) 없이 (v.없다 none, there isn't)밝은 (bright) 달 (moon) 은(s.s)

가슴 (chest, mind)일편 (one piece) 단심 (one mind) 일세 (is) 이 (this)

기상 (strength) 과 (and) 이 (this) 맘 (= 마음 mind) 으로 (with)

충성 (devotion, loyalty) 을 (o.s) 다하여 (with all) 괴로우나 (difficulty)

즐거우나 (delight) 일 (one) 편 (piece) 단(one , single) 심 (mind= 마음) 일세 (is)

No.9 Sam yil Zuhl Song (삼일절노래)

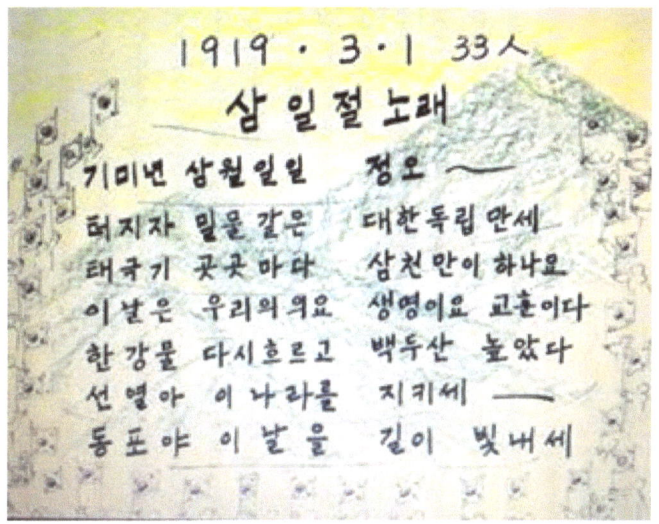

기미년 삼월 일일 정오

Gi-mi-nehn Sam-woul-yil-yil Zuhng-oh

The noon on March 1 st in Gi-Mi year (1919 AD)

터지자 밀물같은

Tuh-zi-za Mil-mul-gat-eun

just like the hgh tide on that time

대한 독립 만세

Dae-han Dog-rimb Man-se

with Korea's Independence Man-Se sounds

태극기 곳곳 마다

Tae-geuk-gi Gots-gots Ma-da

Tae-Geug-Gi was everywhere

삼천만이 하나요

Sam-chun-man-yi Ha-na-yo

Thirty million united in one

이 날은 우리의 의요

YI Nal-eun Wu-ri-euh Euy-yo

This day is our will

생명이요 교훈이다

Saeng-myuhng-yi-yo Gyo-hun-yi-da

and is the life and lesson

한강물 다시 흐르고

han-gang-mul Da-si Heu-reu-go

The Han-River flows again

백두산 높았다

Baeg-du-san Nop-atss-da

Baeg-Du-Mountain getting higher

선열아 이 나라를 지키세

Suhn-yuhl-ah Yi Na-ra-reul Zi-ki-se

Let the Patriots protects this country

동포야 이 날을 기리 빛내세

Dong-po-ya YI Nal-Eul Gi-ri Bich-nae-se

Brothers and sisters , celebrate this day forever.

단어 (Vocabulary)

기미(AD 1919 , a year's name in Korean traditinal calendar which is 단기 dan-gi :

There are 2,333 years difference between 단기 and 서기 suh-gi that is A.D.)

년 (Year) 삼 (Three) 월 (Month) 일(Numeric number one) 일 (Day) 정오 (Noon)

터지자 (As just opened)밀물 (Tide) 같은 (As like) 대한 (Korea) 독립 (Independent)

만세 (a celebrate gesture with stratch two arms up) 태극기 (Korean national Flag)

곳곳 (place after place) meaning of 곳 is the place   Ex. 이곳 yi-gots (Here)

저곳 zuh-gots (There) - 마다 (every each)

삼천만 (30,000,000) 삼 (Three ,3) 천 (Thousand, 1000) 만 (Ten thousand, 10,000)

-- 이 (a subjective suffix   as like -- 가 --은. -- 는)

하나 (one) -- 요 (a definitive suffix as like -다,--이다,-입니다-어요)

* 이 (a indicative word, means * This) 날 (Day) -은 (a subjective suffix) 우리 (Our)

** --의 (a possessive suffix) 의 (the will)

P.S. Some Korean words has the different meanings for same letter

생명(Life) --이요(a definitive suffix) 교훈 (lesson) --이다 (a deffinitive suffix)

한(Han) 강 (River)* 한강 (Han-River streams from the east to the west in Seoul)

물 (Water) 다시 (again) 흐르고 (stream)

백두 (Baek-Du) 산 (Mountain) 백두산 (Baek-du-san is very north of Korera penisula)

높았다 (get Higher) 선열 (patriot) --아 (calling suffix, as like - 야)

이 (this) 나라 (country) 를 (a objective   suffix) 기리 (forever)

지키세 (protect, keep on) 동포 (Fellow, Brithers and Sisters) -- 야 (a calling suffix)

날(day) 을 (a objective s.) 빛네세 (let it shine, celebrate)

No.10 DongNe BangNe Song (동네방네 소문났네 노래)

동네방네 소문났네

동네방네 갔었는데 나들이를 갔었다고
이렁쿵~ 저렁쿵~ 동네방네 소문났네
일 잘하는 큰아기는 나들이도 못가나요
아~ 아~ 음~ 음~ 말도많고 흉도많아
이렁쿵 저렁쿵 요롱쿵 조롱쿵
동네방네 소문났네~.

동네방네 갔었는데   dong-na-bang-ne gatss-uhtss-neun-de

I went to the neiborhood

나들이를 갔었다고   na-deul-i-reul gatss-uhtss-da-go

They said that I went to picnic

이렁쿵 저렁쿵   i-ruh-kung zuh-ruh-kung

this way, that way says so

동네방네 소문났네   dong-ne-bang-ne so-mun-natss-ne

The rumers are all over the neighborhood

일잘하는 큰아기는   il-zal-ha-neun keun-a-gi-neun

I am good worker , daughter -in-law

나들이도 못 가나요 ?   na-deul-i-do mots-ga-na-yo

Why can I not go out ?

아 -- 아 -- 음-- 음--   ah--ah-- eum--eum--

Ah -- ah Eum-eum

말도많고 흉도많아   mal-do-man-go hung-do-manh-a

too much talk and gossip

이렇쿵 저렇쿵 요롱쿵조롱쿵

yi-ruh-kung zuh-ruh-kung yo-roh-kung zo-roh-kung

yi-ruh-kung zuh-ruh-kung yo-roh-kung zo-roh-kung

동네방네 소문났네   dong-ne-bang-ne so-mun-natss-ne

the rumers are all over the neighborhood

단어 (Vocabulary)

동네 방네 (neighborhood) 갔었는데 (had been gone) 나들이 (picnic) 를(a object s)

갔었다고 (saying had gone) 이렇쿵 저렇쿵 (a onometopoeia ; imitating talking)

소문(rumor) 났네 (came out) 일(work) 잘 (good)

큰아기 (daughter-in-law , 며느리 muh-neu-ri,) 는 (s.s.) 나들이 (go out) 도 (even)

못(don't) 가나요 (asking shape of go) 아 ,음 (ah, eum   expression, words,)

말 (talk) 도(even) 많고(a lot) 흉 (gossip)

No.11 Greetings and Introduction (인사와 소개)

안녕하십니까 ?   an-nyeong-ha-simb-ni-gga (sae-yo)

How are you ?

안녕하세요 ?   an-nyeong-ha-sae-yo

How are you ?

제 이름은 조문희입니다   ze i-reum-eun zo-mun-hi-imb-ni-da

My name is Moonhee L. Cho

당신 이름은 무었입니까 ?   dang-sin yi-reum-eun mu-uhtss-imb-ni-gga

What is your name ?

저는 티화니입니다.   zuh-neun ti-fa-ni-imb-ni-da.

I am Tiffany.

티화니는 왜 한국말을 배우려 하십니까 ?

Tiffany-neun wae Han-guk-mal-eul bae-u-ryuh ha-simb-ni-gga

Tiffany, why would you like to learn Korean ?

덕수궁 구경하러 갈려구요.   DuhgSuGung gu-gyeong-ha-ruh gal-ryuh-gu-yo.

I would like to go to see DuhgSu Palace.

그러시면 제가 잘 가르쳐 드리겠읍니다

geu-ruh-si-myuhn ze-ga zal ga-reu-chuh deu-ri-gets-eum-ni-da

Then I would like to teach you well.

감사합니다 선생님.   gam-sa-ham-ni-da suhn-saeng-nim

Thank you teacher.

천만에요   티화니.   chuhn-man-e-yo Tiffany

You are welcome Tiffany.

단어(Vocabulary)

인사(Greetings) 자기(oneself) 소개 (Intoduce) 제 or 저 (humble word of "나 (I))

당신 (you) 이름(Name)은(s.s.) 무었 (What) 입니까(이다 (is)의('s)

의문형 (eu-mun-huhng question shape) - 까 (question suffix, formal shape then 요)

--요 (using to question suffix and a ending of sentence)

안녕하십니까 ? = 안녕하세요 ? (How are you ?)

한국말 (Korean)을(o.s.) 왜 (why) 배우려 (to learn 배우다 learn)

하십니까 =하세요? (intend to do)

덕수궁(DuhgSu Palace in Seoul Korea) 궁 (palace) 구경 (see, sightseeing)

갈려구요 (intend to go) 가다 (Go)

그러 (시)면 (그러면 Then) 의 ('s)높힘말 nop-hin-mal honorable word with '시")

제가 (내가 (I) 의 ('s) 낮춘말 (nat-chun-mal humble word) 잘(well) 가르쳐 (to teach)

가르치다 (teach) 드리겠어요 (give, take care 주다의 높힘말 honorable of 주다)

감사 (thanks) 감사합니다 (Thank you) 대단히 (very)

대단히 감사합니다. Thank you very much. 선생님 (Teacher) 천만에요 (You are welcome)

No.12 The Korean letters and BadChim (한글과 받침)

한글은 자음과 모음으로 구성되었다

Han-geul-eun za-eum-gwa mo-eum-eu-ro gu-suhng-dwae-uhtss-da

Korean letters are consists of the Consonants and Vowels.

자음+모음=글자   consonant + vowel = letter (자, 과, 으, 로, 다)

자음+모음+받침=글자   consonant + vowel+ badchim = letter (한, 글. 은. 음, 성, 었)

글자+글자=낱말   letter + letter = word (한글, 자음, 과, 모음, 으로, 구성 , 되었다)

낱말+조사=절 word + suffix = phrase   (한글은, 자음과 , 모음으로, 구성되었다)

절+절=문장   phrase + phrase = sentence (한글은 자음과 모음으로 구성되었다.)

@ 14 자음 (za-eum Consonants)   ㄱ,ㄴ,ㄷ,ㄹ,ㅁ,ㅂ,ㅅ,ㅇ,ㅈ,ㅊ,ㅋ,ㅌ,ㅍ,ㅎ

ㄱ (gi-yuhg)   ㄴ (ni-eun)   ㄷ (di-geut)   ㄹ (ri-eul)   ㅁ (mi-eum)

ㅂ (bi-eub)   ㅅ (si-ots)   ㅇ (yi-eung)   ㅈ (zi-eut)   ㅊ (chi-eut)

ㅋ (ki-yuhk)   ㅌ (ti-geut)   ㅍ (pi-eup)   ㅎ (hi-eut)

@ 이중자음 (yi-zung-za-eum Double Consonants)

쌍 자음, (ssang) za-eum Twin Consonants   ㄲ, ㄸ,ㅃ, ㅆ,ㅉ,

ㄲ (ssang- gi-yuhg G,K,H mixed sounds, marked with gg)

ㄸ (ssang-di-geud   D,T,H mixed sounds, marked with dd)

ㅃ (ssang-bi-eupb   B,P,H mixed sounds, marked with bb) ,

ㅆ (ssang-si-ots   S,T,H mixed sounds marked with ss)

ㅉ (ssang-zi-eutz   Z,T,S mixed sounds marked with zz)

Ex. 꽃 (ggoht, flower), 꿀 (ggul honey) 뚜껑 (ddu-gguhng lid)

떡 (dduhg, Korean cake)   쌀 (ssal, rice)

\# 혼합자음 (hon-hab-za-eum Mixed Consonants)   ㄳ, ㄵ, ㄶ, ㅄ, ㄺ, ㄻ, ㄼ, ㄽ, ㄾ, ㄿ, ㅀ,

Ex. 넋 nuhgs , 앉 anz 많 man 값 gabs , 닭 dalg, 젊 zuhlm,

밟 balb, 돐 dols, 핥 halt, 읊 eulp, 옳 olh

@ 21 모음 (mo-eum , Vowels)

ㅏ, ㅑ, ㅓ, ㅕ, ㅗ, ㅛ, ㅜ, ㅠ, ㅡ, ㅣ, ㅐ, ㅒ, ㅔ, ㅖ, ㅘ, ㅙ, ㅚ, ㅝ, ㅞ, ㅟ, ㅢ

ㅏ (a), ㅑ (ya), ㅓ (uh), ㅕ (yuh) , ㅗ (o), ㅛ (yo), ㅜ (u), ㅠ (yu),

ㅡ (eu), ㅣ (i), ㅐ (ae), ㅒ (yae). ㅔ (e), ㅖ (ye) ㅘ (wa),

ㅙ (wae), ㅚ (we), ㅝ (wou), ㅞ (weh), ㅟ (wi), ㅢ (euh, euy, ee)

모음은 자음의 소리를 정해준다.   mo-eum-eun za-eum-euy so-ri-reul zuhng-hae-zun-da

The Vowels makes the sounds of Consonants.

P.S. More details on " Korean Alphabets Charts by Moonhee L. Cho"

@ 받침 (bad-chim BadChim)

\# 받침은 무었인가 ?   batd-chim-eun mu-uhtss-in-ga   What is the BadChim ?

\# 원래 받침의 뜻은 상처럼 받쳐주는 물건이다.

woen-rae batd-chim-euy ddeuts-eun sang-chuh-ruhm

batd-chuh-zu-neun mul-guhn-i-da

\# Originary, the BadChim is the supporting thing like a table.

\# 받침은 한글의 자음과 모음 아래에 쓰는 자음이다.

Badchim-eum Han-geul-euy za-eum-gwa mo-eum a-rae-e sseu-neun za-eum-i-da

The BadChim is the consonant that is written under a consonat and a vowel in letter.

무었(what) 원래 (originally) 뜻(mean) 상(table) 처럼 (as like)

받치다 (suport) 물건 (thing) 아래 (under) 쓰는(쓰다) (write)

@ 받침이 없는글자   These letters have **No** Badchim.   batdchim-i uhbs-neun geul-za

예, 기차 (gi-cha Train), 노래 (no-rae, Song) 해 (hae Sun) 머리 (muh-ri, Head)

코(ko,Nose) 귀 (gwi Ear) 다리 (da-ri Leg) 무지게 (mu-zi-ge Rainbow)

과자 (gwa-za Cookie) 바다 (ba-da Sea) 사자 (sa-za Lion) 개 (gae Dog)

@ 받침이 있는 글자 These letters have **Yes** Badchim .   batdchim-i itss-neun geul-za

Ex. 강 (gang, river),밥 (bab, rice) 물 (mul water) 별(byuhl, Star) 달 (dal, Moon) 손 (son, Hand) 넋 (nuhgs Soul Spirit) 닭 (darg Chicken) 딸 (ddal Daughter)

음식 (eum-sig Food) 관강(gwangang, Trip) 비행장 (bi-haeng-zang Airport   )

No.13 Korean;s Basic Sentence Pattern (한글의 기본 문장형식)

@ 문장형식 1 (Sentence Style 1)

@ 주어 zu-uh + 동사 dong-sa (Subject + Verb) shape

예를들면 (ye-reul-deul-muhn for example , 예, Ex.)

나는 잔다. na-neun zan-da I am sleepng.

예. 사과는 맛있다.   sa-gwa-neun mas-iss-da   The apple is delicious.

예. 그녀는 웃는다. geu-nyuh-neun uts-neun-da She is smile.

예. 하늘은 푸르다.   ha-neul-eun pu-reu-da The sky is blue.

단아(Vocabulary)

나 (I) 는 (a subjective suffix) 잔다 (sleep) 사과 (apple) 맛있다 (delicious)

그녀 (she) 웃는다 (smile) 하늘 (sky) 은 (a sujective suffix) 푸르다 (blue)

@ 문장형식 2 (Sentence Style 2)

@ 주어 zu-uh + 목적어 mog-zuhg-uh + 동사 dong-sa (Subject + Object + Verb) Shape

예. 그는 청소를 한다   Geu-neun Chung-so-reul Han-da

He is cleaning.

예. 당신은 노래를 부른다   Dang-sin-eun No-rae-reul Bu-reun-da

You   are singing.

예. 언니는 수영을 한다   Uhn-ni-neun Su-young-eul Han-da

Older sister is swimming.

예. 오빠는 배구를 한다   O-bba-neun bae-gu-reul han-da

Older brother is playing volleyball.

단어 (Vocabulary)

한국말 (Korean) 기본 (basic) 문장(sentence) 형식(style) 주어(subject) 목적어 (object)

동사 (verb) 나 (I) 그 (he) 당신 (you) 공부(study) 청소 (cleaning) 노래 (sing)

수영 (swimming) 을 (objective suffix, o.s.) 배구(volleyball) 를 (o.s.) 한다(doing play)

@ 문장형식 3 (Sentence Style 3)

@ 형용사 hyuhng-yong-sa +주어 zu-uh +목적어 mog-zuhg-uh +부사 bu-sa +동사 dong-sa (Adjective+Subject+Object+Adverb+Verb)

예. 즐거운 친구가 나를 크게 부른다.   zeul-guh-un chin-gu-ga na-reul keu-ge bu-reun da

Joyful friend calling me loudly.

예. 하늘의 별은 왜 저렇게 반짝이나 ?   ha-neul-euy byuhl-eun wae zuh-ruhh-ge ban-zzag-i-na

Why does the stars of sky so shines ?

예. 우리 아들은 정구를 참 잘한다 .   wu-ri a-deul-eun zuhng-gu-reul cham zal-han-da

Our son plays tennis very well.

예. 큰 동물원에는 귀여운 동물이 많다.   keun dong-mul-woun-e-neun gwi-yuh-wun dong-mul-i manh-da

The big zoo has many cute animals.

예. 아름다운 언니는 수영을 멋있게 한다   a-reum-da-un uhn-ni-neun su-yuhng-eul muhts-itss ge-han-da

Beautiful sister swims stylishly.

단어

즐거운 (joyful)친구(friend)가 (a calling suffix) 나(I) 를(objective s.)크게(loudly) 부른다(call)

왜 (why)하늘(sky)의(possessive s.) 별(star)은(s.s.) 저렇게 (so) 반짝(shine) 이나(a qustion shape word ,?)

우리 (our) 아들 (son) 은 (s.s.) 정구 (tennis)를(o.s.)참 (very)잘(well)큰(big)동물원(Zoo)에는(at)

귀여운(cute) 동물(animal)이 (s.s.) 많다 (many) 아름다운(beautiful)멋있게 (stylish)

who (a connecting word that indicates the subjective person 주어 된 사람을 가르키는 접속사)

No.14 HanGeul's Classifications (한글의 품사구분)

@ 명사 (myuhng-sa   Noun)

비행기 (bi-haeng-gi   Airplane)해 (hae   Sun) 달 (dal   Moon) 차 (cha   Car or Tea)

돈 (don   Money) 식당 (sig-dang   Restaurant) 학교 (hag-gyo   School)

학생 (hag-saeng student) 버스 (buh-seu Bus) 책(cheg Book) 연필 (yuhn-pil pencil)

점심 (zuhm-sim Lunch) 친구(chin-gu Friend) 등등 (deung-deung etc.   a sign with .. .)

@ 대명사   (dae-myuhng-sa   Pronoun)

그 (geu The) 당신 (dang-sin You)그곳 (geu-gots   There) 그것 (geu-guhts It)

어디 (uh-di   Where) 누구 (nu-gu Who) 이곳 (i-gots   Here) 저기 (zuh-gi There)

@ 동사 (dong-sa   verb)

움직인다 (um-zig-in-da   Move) 걷다 (guhd-da Walk)가다 (ga-da   Go = 간다 gan-da)

오다 (o-da   Come = 온다 on-da) 운다 (un-da   Cry = 울다   ul-da) 웃다 (uts-da Laugh)

춤추다 (chum-chu-da   Dance) 뛰다 (ddwi-da   Run)   말하다 (mal-ha-da speak) . . .

@ 형용사 (hyung-yong-sa Adjective)

좋은(zoh-eun   Good, Nice) 예쁜 (yae-bbeun Pretty) 아름다운(a-reum-da-un Beautiful)

귀여운(gwi-yuh-un Cute) 우아한 (wu-a-han graceful)멋있는 (mus-is-neun neat ,cool)

큰 (keun Big) 작은 (zag-eun Small) 비싼 (bi-ssa Expensive) 싼 (ssan Cheap)

많은 (manh-eun A Lot) 달콤한(dal-kom-han Sweet) 짠(zzan Salty)

매운 (mae-un Hot) 맛있는 (mats-itss-neun Delicious) 멋있는(muhs-its-neun Elegant)

기쁜(gi-bbeun Delight) 바쁜 (ba-bbeun Busy) 짧은 (zzal-eun Short) 긴 (gin Long)

대단히(dae-dan-hi Very)친절한 (chin-zuhl-han Kind)감사한 (gam-sa-han Thankful)

정다운 (zuhng-da-un Friendly) 반가운 (ban-ga-un Glad) 즐거운 (zeul-guh-un Joyful)

빛나는 (bitch-na-neun Shiny) 가벼운 (ga-byuh-un Light) 무거운 (mu-guh-un Heavy)

뜨거운 (ddeuh-guh-un Hot) 차가운(cah-ga-un Cold) 조용한 (zo-yong-han quite)

시끄러운 (si-ggeu-ruh-un noisy) 다정한 (da-zuhng-han compassionate) 친절한 (kind   )

@ 부사   (bu-sa Adverb)

잘 (zal Well) 빨리(bbal-ri Hurry) 천천히 (chun-chun-hi Slowly)

갑자기 (gab-za-gi Suddenly) 즐겁게 (zeul-guhb-ge Joyful)

기쁘게 (gi-bbeu-ge Delightly) 조심스럽게 (zo-sim-seu-ruhb-ge Carefully)

자세하게 (za-se-ha-ge Detailed) 힘차게 (him-cha-ge Strongly)

공손하게 (ging-son-ha-ge Politely) 조용히 (zo-yong-hi Quietly)

똑바르게 (ddog-ba-reu-ge Rightly , Straightly)

완전하게 (wan-zuhn-ha-ge Completely) 비밀히 (bi-mil-hi Secretly)

정직하게 (zuhng-zig-ha-ge Honestly)

@ 감탄사   (gam-tam-sa Exclamations   )

기쁠때 (gi-BBeul-ddae When Joyful)

아 (a Ah) 와아(wa-a Wha) 오 (o Oh))하아 (ha-a Hah) 어머나 (uh-muh-na)

아이고 좋겠다 (a-i-go-zoh-getss-da How glad you are) . . .

슬플때 (seul-peul-ddae   When sorrowful)

에구나 (e-gu-na) 쯔쯔(zzeu-zzeu) 어떡해 (uh-dduhg-hae what shall we do)

아 안됐다 (a-an-daetss-da Oh sorry) 저런 (zuh-ruhn How that)

저런일이 (How that happen). . .

@ 조사 (zo-sa   postposition Particles)

\# 글자 앞에 붙이는 접두어 (Prefix) geul-za ap-e but-i-neun zuhb-du-uh

The prefix that comes in front of the letter

\# 글자 뒤에 붙이는 접미어 (Suffix) geul-za dwi-e but-i-neun zuhb-mi-uh

The suffix that comes at the end of the letter

@ 접두어   (zuhb-du-uh Prefix)

\# 부정 접두어 (bu-zuhng zuhb-du-uh Denial Prefix)

1. 안 (an No, Not yet) = 불 (bul) = 부 (bu)

예, 당신은 그를 찬성 하십니까 ?   Would you agree with him ?

dang-sin-eun geu-reul chan-suhng ha-simb-ni-gga

예, 아니요 찬성 안합니다. (불찬성합니다)   No, I do not agree (disagree).

a-ni-yo chan-suhng an-hamb-ni-da (bul-chan-suhng-hamb-ni-da)

당신 (You) 은 (a Subject s.) 그 (he) 을 (a Objective suffix.) 그를 (him)

찬성 (agree) \# 하십니까 (하시다 의 의문형   the question shape of 하시다)

\# 의문형 조사   (eu-mun-huhng zo-sa Question Suffix   -- 까 (gga   )

예, 안녕하십니까 (an-nyuhng-ha-simb-nigga How are you ?)

예, 당신 이름은 무엇입니까 ? (dang-sin-i-reum-eun mu-uhts-imb-ni-gga)

What is your name ?

\# 하시다 (하다의 높힘말   the polite shape of 하다 does)

\# 안 (the denial prefix) \# 찬성 안합니다 (does not agree)= 불찬성 합니다 (disagree)

\# Polite Shape means 높힘형 (nop-hin-hyung) ,

the Original Shape means 원형 (woun-hyuhng)

보통 원형에다" 시 " 또는 "신 " 을 붙여 높힌말로 쓴다

bo-tong woun-hyuhng-e-da 'si" ddo-neun "sin eul but-yuh nop-hin-mal-ro sseun-da

Usually, using the polite word adding "시" or "신" to the original shape.

Except 먹다 (muhg-da eat) " s 높힌말 is 잡수시다 (zab-su-si-da)

not 먹신다 (muhg-sin-da)

ex (예). 원형 (Original Shape)   높힘말 (Polite Shape)

하다 (ha-da   Do, Does) ---   하신다 (ha-sin-da)

오다 (o-da   Come) ---   오신다 (o-sin-da)

가다 (ga-da   Go)   ---   가신다 (ga-sin-da)

보다 (bo-da   See) ---   보신다 (bo-sin-da)

일하다 (il-ha-da   Work) --- 일하신다 (il-ha-sin-da)

웃다 (uts-da Laugh) ---   웃으신다 (uts-eu-sin-da)

울다 (ul-da Cry)   ---   울으신다 (ul-eu-sin-da)

먹다 (muhg-da Eat) --- 잡수시다 (zab-su-si-da)

걷다 (guhd-da Walk) --- 걸으신다 (guhl-eu-si-da)

자다 (za-da   Sleep) --- 주무신다 (zu-mu-si-da)

깨다 (ggae-da Wake up) --- 깨신다 (ggae-sin-da) . . .

예, 저는 이 주제에 가부를 묻겠습니다

I would like to ask yes or no if you agree or disagree about this subject ?

zuh-neun i zu-ze-e ga-bu-reul mud-gess-eum-nida

예, 찬성하시면 당신의 손을 들으세요. Please rase your hand up if you are agree.

chan-suhng-ha-si-myuhn dang-sin-euy son-eul deul-eu-se-yo

저 (I) 는 (subjective s.) 이 (this) 주제 (suject) 에 (indicating suffix)

가 (agree, yes)부 (disagree, no) 를 (objective suffix)

묻겠습니마 (ask, polte shape of 묻다) 찬성(agree) 하시면 (if you do)

손(hand) 을 (objective suffix) 들으세요 (rase up, polite shape of 들마)

2. 못 (mots   Won't, don't can't)

예, 너 , 저리로 가   nuh, zuh-ri-ro ga   You, go to there.

예, 싫어, 나 못 가.   silh-uh, na mots-ga   No way, I won't go.

너 (You) 저리 (There) 로(To)가 (Go) 싫어 (No way) 나 (I) 못 (Won't)

복귀접두어 (bog-gwi-zuhb-du-uh   Return Prefix)

되 (dwoe Back to , Return)

예, 당신에게 보낸 소포가 어제 나에게 되 돌아왔다 ,

dang-sin-e-ge bo-naen so-po-ga   uh-ze na-e-ge dwue dol-a-wat-da

The parcel that I sent to you was returned to me yesterday.

당신(you) 에게 (to) 보낸 (sent) 소포 (parcel)가 (subjective s.)

어제 (yesterday)나 (me)에게(to)되 (back)돌아왔다 (return)

반복접두어 (ban-bog-zuhb-du-uh Repetitive Prefix)

재 (zae   Repeat , Again)

재검사 (zae-guhm-sa   Reinspection), 재수출 (zae-su-chul Reexport)

재수입 (zae-su-ib Reimport), 재시험 (zae-si-huhm Retest) 등등.

@ 접미어 (zuhb-mi-uh Suffix)

주격 (zu-gyuhg Subjective) (..는 ..은 .이는 ..이 ..가. .이가)

1.-- 는 (neun)   After the word or name that ends with No BatdChim

예 그는, 나는, 저는, 영자는, 순희는, 병수는, 규대는, 친구는, 바다는,

2 -- 은 (eun)   After the word or ending with Yes BatdChim

예 당신은, 선생님은, 산은, 구름은, 장미꽃은, 낙엽은, 바림은

3. -- 이는 (i-neun)   After the names that end with Yes BatdChim

예 금순이는, 영옥이는, 숙현이는, 완섭이논, 철진이는, 구철이는

4. -- 이 (i)   After the word that ends with Yes BatdChim

예 사람이, 정신이, 하늘이, 구름이, 닭이, 창문이, 바람이, 강물이,

5. -- 가 (ga)   After the word that ends with No BatdChim

예 내가, 정자가, 나무가, 무지게가, 자전거가, 코가, 증거가

6. -- 이가 (i-ga)   After the name that ends with Yes BatdChim

예 정숙이가, 규남이가, 성운이가, 사랑이가, 혜인이가, 금옥이가,

목적격 (mogzuhg-gyuhg Objective) (--를. --을 ,--이를)

1. -- 를 (reul)   After the word or name that ends with No BatdChim

예, 학생은 공부를 배우러 학교에 갑니다

hag-saeng-eun gung-bu-reul bae-u-ruh hag-gyo-e gab-ni-da

The student is going to school to learn.

학생(student) 은(subjective suffix,)   공부(study) 를(objective suffix)

배우러 (for learn) 학교(school) 에(to = 로 ro) 갑니다(going)

2. -- 을(eul)   After the word that ends with Yes BatdChim

예, 그는 학교가 끝난 후에 수영을 합니다.

geu-neun hag-gyo-ga ggeut-nan-hu-e su-yuhng-eul hab-ni-da

He is swimming after school.

3.-- 이를 (i-reul)   After the name that ends with Yes BatdChim

예,, 나는 전철에서 명숙이를 만났습니다.

na-neun zuhn-chuhl-e-suh myuhng-sug-i-reul man-nass-eum-ni-da

I met Myuhng-suk at subway..

나 (I) 는 (s.s) 잔철 (subway) 에서(at) 명숙(one of name) 이를 (o.s.)

만났습니다 (met, past shape 과거형 gwa-guh-hyung of meet 만나다. present shape, 현재형 hyun-zae)

@ 복수격 조사 (bog-su-gyuhg zosa (plural suffix)

. --- 들 (deul)

예 ex 나무들 (trees), 학생들(students), 나비들 (butterflies), 집들 (houses),

생선들 (fishes), 꽃들 flowers) 여자들 (women)...

@ 방향격 조사 (bang-hyang-gyuhg   zo-sa Directive suffix)   --로,--으로,,--에게

1 -- 로 (ro To place)

After the word that ends with   No BatdChim

이리로(i-ri-ro   to here) 가게로 (ga-ge-ro   to the store)학교로 (hag-gyo-ro to the school) 등등.(etc.)

2.-- 으로 (eu-ro To place)

After the word that ends with Yes BatdChim

이곳으로 (i-gots-eu-ro to here) 저곳으로(zuh-gots-eu-ro to there)

방으로 (bang-eu-ro to the room) 창문으로(chang-mun-eu-ro to the window)..

3 -- 에게 (e- ge, to who)

After the word that has No or Yes BatdChim

나에게 (na-e-ge, to me) 딸에게 (ddal-e-ge, to daughter)

그들에게 (geu-deul-e-ge to them)

4. -- 께 (gge To)

After an honorable or upper person

선생님께 (suhn-saeng-nim-gge to teacher) 부모님께 (bu-mo-nim-gge to parent)

당신께 (dang-sin-gge to you) # You means 당신 (dang-sin   Polite way   )

너 (nuh Impolite way of you , using between friends or younger person)

@ 위치격 조사 (wi-chi-gyuhg zo-sa   Locative Suffix) . .에. .에서 ...부터 ...까지

1. --에 (e At)

여기에 (yuh-gi-e At here) 저기에, (zuh-gi-e At there)

그 곳에 (geu gos-e   over there) 하늘에 (ha-neul-e At the sky)

예, 하늘에 무지게가 있어요   The rainbow is in the sky

ha-neul-e mu-zi-ge-ga itss-uh-yo

하늘(sky) 에(at) 무지게(rainbow)가 (subjective .s) 있어요(is)

2 --에서 (e-suh   At or From)

예, 정거장 디에서 만나요 See you at the station D.

zuhng-guh-zang di-e-suh man-na-yo

정거장 (station) 디 (D) 에서 (at) 만나요 (see you , meet you)

예, 당신은 어느 나라에서 왔어요 ? Which country are you from ?

dang-sin-eun uh-neu na-ra-e-suh watss-uh-yo

당신(you)은 (s.s.)어느 (which)나라 (country)에서(from) 왔어요(came ? past shape of 오다)

3.. -- 부터 (bu-tuh From)

여기부터 (yuh-gi-bu-tuh from here) 저기부터(zuh-gi-bu-tuh from there

집부터 (zib-bu-tuh from house)

4 . -- 까지 (gga-zi To)

여기까지 (yuh-gi-gga-zi to here) 저기까지 (zuh-gi-gga-zi to there)

학교까지 (hag-gyo-gga-zi to school)

예, 여기부터 저기까지 걸어 갑시다 Let's walk from here to there

yuh-gi-butuh zuh-gi-gga-zi guhl-uh-gab-si-da

예, 집에서 학교까지 얼마나 멉니까 ? How far from house to school ?

zib-e-suh hag-gyo-gga-zi uhl-ma-na muhm-ni-gga

걸어 = 걷다 (walk) 집 (house) 학교(school) 까지 (to)

얼마나 (how much) 멉니까 (멀다's 의문형 question shape)

@ 소유격 조사 (so-u-guhg zo-sa   Possessive Suffix)

1. -- 의 (euh --'s)

나의 (na-euh My) 당신의 (dang-sin-euh Your)

그 남자의 (geu nam-za-euh His) 그 여자의 (geu yuh-za-euh Her)

예, 당신이 내 곁에 있으면 내 마음이 즐거워요.

If you are near me , my mind is delighted.

dang-sin-yi nae gyuht-e yits-eu-myhn nae ma-eum-i zeul-guh-wou-yo

당신 (you) 이 (s.s) 내 (나의) (me, my) 곁에 (near, beside)

있으면 (if are) 마음 (mind) 이 (s.s) 즐거워요 (delight, joy)

예, 그 남자의 소망은 그 여자의 행복이예요

His hope is her happiness

geu-nam-za-euh so-mang-eun geu yuh-za-euh haeng-bog-i-ye-yo

그 (the) 남자 (man, he) 의 ('s)= his 소망 (hope) 은 (s.s)

여자 (woman, she) 그 여자의 (her) 행복 (happiness) 이예요 (is)

2. -- 의 것 (euh guhts --'s Belong)

나의 것 (na-euh guhts Mine) 너의 것 (nuh-euh guhts Your's)

예 이 것은 나의 것이고 저 것은 너의 것입니다

This is mine that is your's.

i guhys-eun na-euh guhts i-go zuh-guhts-eun nuh-euh guhts-im-ni-da

이 (this) 것 (thing) 은 (s.s)=this 나의 (my) 것 (thing)=mine

저 (that) 것(thing) 은(s.s)= that   너의 (your)것(thing)=yours

@ 한정격 조사 (han-zuhng-gyuhg zo-sa Limitation Suffix) -- 만큼 - 처럼 --같이 --정도

1. 만큼 (man-keum As much as)

예. 우리 학교도 당신 학교 만큼 커요. u-ri hag-gyo-do dang-sin hag-gyo man-keum kuh-yo

Our school is big as much as yours.

2. 처럼 (chuh-ruhm   As like as)

예 당신의 얼굴은 달처럼 밝아요 .dang-sin-euh uhl-gul-eun dal-chuh-ruhm barg-a-yo

Your face is bright like Moon.

3. 같이 (gat-i   As same as)

예 당신의 차는 제것하고 똑 같아요. dang-sin-euh cha-neun ze-guhs-ha-go ddog-gat-a-yo

Your car looks the same as mine.

4. 정도 (zuhng-do About)

예 여기서 저기까지는 2 마일 정도 되어요. yuh-gi-suh zuh-gi-gga-zi-neum

yi-ma-il zuhng-do doe-uh-yow

It is about 2 miles from here to there .

\# 주목격 (zu-mog-gyuhg Atentional) ; 호칭 (ho-ching Calling suffix)

(the suffix after persons name when you call their name)

--야 --아 --양 --군 --씨 --선생 --님

1 -- 야 (ya) 자기보다 어린사람 또는 친구을 부를 때, 받침이없는 글자로 끝나는 이름에 붙인다.

To younger person than me or friend's name that has No BatdChim ending word like these names

예 영자야 수지야 규대야 진수야 금희야, 순희야, 문희야, 길수야. 나비야

2. --아 (a) 자기보다 어린사람 또는 친구를 부를때, 받침이 있는 글자로 끝나는 이름에 붙인다

To younger person than me or friend's name that has Yes BatdChim ending word like these names

예 금순아 영철아 완섭아 혜인아 규식아 , 성운아, 사랑아, 미림아, 명숙아

나 (I, me) 보다 (than) 어린(younger) 사람 (person)

친구 (friend) 에게 (to) 이름 (name) 끝나는 (ending)

3. -- 양 (yang MIss)   성숙한 숙녀를 정중히 부를때

To grown young lady with politely or officially.(Usually with last name= full name.)

예 이 문희양, 김 숙자양 , 정 태임양,, 신 정숙양

4. -- 군 (gun Mr.)   To grown young man with the politetly or officially.

예 이 규대군, 김 영수군, 조 진길군, 함 규식군

5. -- 씨 (ssi)   To grown man and woman with the polite or officially

예 이 원영씨, 배 국향씨, 송 효석씨 이 희창씨.

6. -- 선생 (suhn-saeng) To grown man and woman with respectations.

예 고 광림 선생, 이 후경 선생. 유 효경선생, , 배 진영 선생,

7. -- 님 (nim) To grown person with the very respect to them or their job

선생님 (suhn-saeng-nim, Teacher) 부모님 (bu-mo-nim Parent)

목사님 (mog-sa-nim, Pastor) 사장님 (sa-zang-nim Chairman)

8. -- 각하 (gag-ha)   To very highest person like the president

대통령 각하 (dae-tong-ryuhng gag-ha   Majestic President)

@ 접속어   (zuhb-sog-uh Conjunctive words)

그리고 (geu-ri-go And) # 그러나 (geu-ruh-na But) # 역시 (yuhg-si Also)

.# 그러므로 (geu-ruh-meu-ro Therefore) #그때문에 (geu-ddae-mun-e Because of)

그뿐만아니라 (geu-bbun-man-a-ni-rta Not only but also)

이와같이 (i-wa-gat-i Thus) # 마찬가지로 .(ma-chan-ga-zi-ro As well as)

@ 지시어   (zi-si-uh   Indicating words)

이것 (i-guhts This)   #. 저것 (zuh-guhts That) # 그것 (geu-guhts It)

어느것 (uh-neu-guhts Which)   # 아무것 (a-mu-guhts Any, Anything   )

@ 의태어 (euh-tae-uh Mimesis) (The words that describes the shapes   )

예, 방실방실 bang-sil bang-sil , 아장아장 a-zang a-zang ,복실복실 bog-sil bog-sil, . . .

@ 의성어 (euh-suhng-uh Onomatopoeia) (The words that describes the sounds)

예, 쾅쾅쾅 kwang-kang-kwang, 짝짝 zzaeg-zzaeg , 두근두근 du-geun-du-geun, ...

p.s. more details on No. 17. 의태어와 의성어

@ 수사 (su-sa Numeral)

정수 (zuhng-su Numbers = 숫자 suts-za)

1 2 3 4 5 6 7 8 9 10 11 12 13 14 15 16 17 18 19 20 ---- 100 1000 10000 1000000 . . .

서수 (suh-su) for writing and reading   # 셈수. (sem-su)   for counting

숫자 (numbers)	서수 (for read)	셈수 (for count)
1	일 il	하나 ha-na
2	이 i	둘 dul or du
3	삼 sam	셋 sets
4	사 sa	넷 nets
5	오 o	다섯 da-suhts
6	육 yug	여섯 yuh-suhts
7	칠 chil	일곱 il-gob
8	팔 pal	여덟 yuh-duhlb
9	구 gu	아홉 a-hob
10	십 sib	열 yuhl
11	십일 sib-il	열하나 yuhl-ha-na
12	십이 sib-i	열둘 yuhl-dul
13	십삼 sib-sam	열셋 yuh-sets
14	십사 sib-sa	열넷 yuhl-nets
15	십오 sib-o	열다섯 yuhl-da-suhts

16	십육	sib-yug	열여섯	yuhl-yuh-suhts
17	십칠	sib-chil	열일곱	yuhl-il-gob
18	십팔	sib-pal	열여덟	yuhl-yuh-duhlb
19	십구	sib-gu	열아홉	yuhl-a-hob
20	이십	i-sib	스물	seu-mul
21	이십일	i-sib0il	스물하나	seu-mul-ha-na
22	이십이	i-sib-i	스물둘	seu-mul-dul
30	삼십	sam-sib	사른	suh-reun
31	삼십일	sam-sib-il	서른하나	suh-reun-ha-na
40	사십	sa-sb	마흔	ma-heun
41	사십일	sa-sib-il	마흔하나	ma-heun-ha-na
50	오십	o-sib	쉬흔	seui-heun
60	육십	yug-sib	예슨	ye-seun
70	칠십	chil-sib	이른	a-heun
80	팔십	pal-sib	여든	yuh-deun
90	구십	gu-sib	아흔	a-heun
100	백	baeg	백	baeg
101	백일	baeg-il	백하나	baeg-ha-na
102	백이	baeg-i	백둘	baeg-dul
200	이백	i-baeg	이백	i-baeg
201	이백일	i-baeg-il	이백하나	i-baeg-ha-na
202	이백이	i-baeg-i	이백둘	i-baeg-dul

222	이백이십이	i-baeg-i-sib-i	이백스물둘	i-baeg-seu-mul-dul
1000	천	chun	천	chun
5555	오천오백오십오		오천오뱃싁흔다삿	
	o-chun-o-baeg-o-sib-o		o-chun-o-baeg-seui-heun-da-suhts	
10000	만	man	만	man
100000	십만	sib-man	십만	sib-man
1000000	백만	baeg-man	백만	baeg-man
100000000	억	uhg	억	uhg

예문 (ye-mun Example Sentences)   ps. 예 (ye, example, ex.)

예, 오늘은 12월 12일 입니다   0-neul-eun sib-i-woul sib-i-il imb-n-0da

Today is December 12th.

오늘(today) 은(s.s.) 12월 (month)= December 일 (day) 입니다 (is)

예, 나는 12 살 입니다 .   na-neun yuhl-du sal imb-ni-da

I am 12 years old. 나 (I) 는 (s.s.) 살 (years old) 입니다 (am)

예, 일년에는 12 달이 있습니다   il-nyuhn-e-neun yuhl-du dal-i utss-seum-ni-da

One year has 12 months = 12 months are in a year

일(one , a) 년(year) 에는(in) 달(month) 있습니다(are)

예, 지금은 오후 12 시 입니다   zi-geum-eun o-hu yuhl-du-si imb-ni-da

Now is p.m. 12 O'clock = It is 12 p.m.

지금 (now) 오후 (afternoon , p.m.= Post meridiem in Latin)

시(time) # 오전 (o-zuhn   before noon   a.m. = Ante meridiem in Latin)

예, 하루에는 24 시간이 있습니다   ha-ru-e-neun i-sib-sa si-gan-i itss-seum-ni-da

One day has 24 hours.   하루 (one day)   시간 (hour)

예, 한 시간에는 60 분이 있습니다   han si-gan-e-neun yug-sib bun-i itss-seum-ni-da

One hour has 60 minutes.   한 (one) 시간 (hour) 분(minute)

예, 일 분에는 60 초가 있습니다   il bun-e-neun yug-sib cho-ga itss-seum-ni-da

One minute has 60 seconds.   일 (1, one . a) 초 (second)

No.15 The Family Relations (가족관계)

할아버지 (hal-ah-buh-zi Grandfather) 할머니 (hal-muh-ni Grandmother)

친할아버지 (chin-hal-a-buh-zi Father's father)

친할머니 (chin-Hal-Muh-Ni Father's mother)

외할아버지 (woe-hal-a-buh-zi Mother's father)

외할머니 (woe-Hal-muh-ni Mother's mother)

친(chin) means Father's side , 외 (woe) means Mother's side.

아버지(a-buh-zi Father) 어머니 (uh-muh-ni Mother)

부모 (bu-mo Parent   부 (bu)   means Father , 모 (mo) means Mother)

아빠 (a-bba Dad) 엄마(uhm-ma Mom) 오빠 (o-bba Older brother of her)

형(hyhung Older brother of him) 언니(uhn-ni Older sister of her)

누나 (nu-na Older sister of him) 형제 (hyung-ze Brothers) 자매 (za-mae Sisters)

동생(dong-saeng Younger than me) 여동생 (yuh-dong-saeng Younger sister)

남동생(nam-dong-saeng Younger brother)

여 means Female (Ex. 여자 Yuh-za ; Woman) 남 means Male (Ex. 남자 Nam-za ; Man)

큰아빠 (keun-a-bba Father's older brother) = 큰숙부

큰엄마 (keun-uhm-ma Wife of father's old brother) =큰숙모

작은아빠 (zag-eun-a-bba Father's younger brother) =작은숙부

작은엄마 (zag-eun-uhm-ma Wife of father's younger brother)=작은숙모

큰 means Older or Big ,   작은 means Younger or Small

시집 (si-zib Husband's home)=시가 (si-ga) 시 means Husband's family

시집가다 (si-zib-ga-da Going to husband's home, thus, marrige)

시아버지(si-a-buh-zi Father-in-law) 시어머니 (si-uh-muh-ni Mother-in-law)

시누 (이) (si-nu-i sister of husband) 큰시누 (older 시누) 작은시누 (younger 시누)

시숙(님) (Si-sug-nim Husband's brother 큰시숙(older),

시동생 (si-dong-saeng Younger husband's brother 작은시숙)

처가 (chuh-ga Wife's home = 친정(집 chin-zuhng-zib) 처 means wife

장인 (zang-in Father of wife) 장모님 (zang-mo-nim Mother of wife)

처남(chuh-nam Brother of wife) 처남댁 (chuh-nam-daeg Wife of 처남)

처형 (chuh-hyung Older sister of wife) 처동서 (chuh-dong-suh Husband of 처형, brother-in-law)

처제(chuh-ze Younger sister of wife) 처동서 (chuh-dong-suh Husband of 처제)

동서 means Spouse of brother or sister-in-law's

큰동서 (keun-dong-suh Older 동서) 작은동서 (zag-eun-dong-suh Younger 동서)

맏동서 (matd-dong-suh Oldest 동서) 맏 means Oldest one in family

막내동서 (mag-nae-dong-suh Youngest 동서   막내 means Youngest one in family   )

형(님) (hyung-nim His older brother) 형수(hyung-su Wife of his old brother)

매부 (mae-bu Husband of her older sister) 매형 (mae-hyung Husband of his older sister)

매제 (mae-ze Husband of his younger sister)

형부 (hyung-bu Husband of her older sister)

제부(ze-bu Husband of her younger sister)

친숙부 (chin-sug-bu Father's brother=친삼촌 Chin-sam-chon, Uncle)

친숙모(chin-sug-mo Wife of father's brother, Aunt) 친 is Father's side 외 is Mother's side

외숙부(woe-sug-bu Mother's brother = 외삼촌 woe-sam-chon)

외숙모(woe-sug-mo Wife of mother's brother = 외작은엄마)

새엄마 (sae-uhm-ma Step-mother = 계모 gye-mo)

새아빠 (sae-a-bba Step-father = 계부 gye-bu) 새 means New

첩 (chub Second wife)   서자 (suh-za Son with second wife)

의붓자식(euh-buts-za-sig Adopted child) = 양자 (Yang-za)

외아들(woe-a-deul Only son) 외동딸(woe-dong-ddal Only daughter) 외 means Only

맏자식 (마지)(mad-za-sig (ma-zi Oldest kid) 맏아들 (mad-a-deul oldest son)

맏딸 mad-ddal oldest daughter) 막 (내) 동이 (mag-ne-dong-i Youngest kid)

동서지간 (dong-suh-zi-gan Relationship between sisters-in-law or brothers-in-law)

이모 (Yi-mo Mother's sister) 이모부 (Yi-mo-bu Husband of 이모)

고모 (go-mo Father's Sister) 고모부 (go-mo-bu Husband's of 고모)

큰이모(keun-yi-mo Older 이모) 작은이모 (zack-eun-yi-mo Younger 이모)

큰고모(keun-go-mo Older 고모) 작은고모 (zack-eun-go-mo Younger 고모)

삼촌(sam-chon Brother of Parent) 작은삼촌 , 큰삼촌

친가(chin-ga Father side family) 외가 (woe-ga Mother side family)

사촌 (sa-chon Cousin) 큰사촌 (Older 사촌) 작은사촌 (Younger 사촌)

친사촌(chin-sa-chon Father's side cousin) 외사촌(woe-sa-chon Mother's side cousin)

시사촌 (si-sa-chon Husband's cousin) 시 means husband's side

총각 (chong-gag Bachelor) 처녀 (chuh-nyuh Bachelorette

규수 (gyu-su Woman ready for marriage)

천생연분 (chun-saeng-yuhn-bun Perfect maching person)

사랑 (sa-rang Love) 신랑 (sin-rang Groom) 신부 (sin-bu Bride)

약혼 (yag-hon Engagement)결혼식 (gyuhl-hon-sig Wedding)

백년가약 (baeg-nyun-ga-yag Promise for 100 years together)

금혼식 (geum-hon-sig 50 years anniversary) 부부 (bu-bu Husband and wife, couple)

아내 (ah-nae Wife) (처 Chuh means wife on the paper and for calling too)

otherwise 각씨(gag-ssi) 색씨(saeg-ssi) 부인 (bu-in)

애기엄마 (ae-gi-uhm-ma, means mother of baby) 마누라 (ma-nu-ra)

안방마님 (an-bang-ma-nim means woman in the masteroom)

집사람 (zib-sa-ram, person who is inside house) 안사람 (an-sa-ram,)

여편네 (Yhuh-pyuhn-ne, Person who is besideof him).

남편 (nam-pyun Husband) (부 bu means husband on the paper)

otherwise 신랑(sin-rang) 부군 (bu-gun) 낭군님 (nang-gun-nim)

서방님 (suh-bang-nim) 애기아빠 (ae-gi-ah-bba, means father of baby)

바깥양반 (ba-ggat-yang-ban, means good person who is outside).

부부 (bu-bu Couple , Husband and Wife in formal) 여보 (yuh-bo Calling word brtween husband and wife)

당신 (dang-sin sane as 여보 , Actually 당신 means you)

임자 (yim-za   some husband call his wife 임자 means Owner)

사돈(sa-don Relations between husband's and wife's parents)

바깥사돈(ba-ggats-sa-don Father of son or daughter-in-law) 안사돈(an-sa-don Mother of son or daughter-in-law)

사위 (sa-wi Son-in-law) 며느리 (myuh-neu-ri Daughter-in-law)

색씨 (seag-ssi Young married lady or any young person who looks like married)

아기 (a-gi Baby) 아들 (a-deul Son) 딸 (ddal Daughter)

자녀 (za-nyuh cildren, kids) 자 means Son , 녀 (여) means Daughter

손자 (son-za Grand son) 손녀 (son-nyuh Grandaughter)

증손자 (zeung-son-za Great grandson) 증손녀 (zeung-son-nyuh Great grandaughter)

친손자(chin-son-za Son's son) 외손자(Woe-son-za Daughter's son)

친손녀(chin-son-nyuh Son's) 외손녀 (woe-son-nyuh Daughter's)

큰아기 (keun-a-gi, when father-in-law called his daughter-in-law)

도련님(do-ryuhn-nim husband's unmarried younger brither)

시누님 (SI-nu-nim Husband's older sister) 새언니 (sae-uhn-ni Wife of her older brother)

사돈의 팔촌 (sa-don-euy Pal-chon The 8th generations of in-law's ;so means a kind of family)

아저씨(a-zuh-ssi Middle aged man who has no relations)

선생님 (sun-saeng-nim Any honorable person 선생님 means teacher)

아주머니 (a-zu-muh-ni Mid age woman who has no relations) 사모님 (sa-mo-nim Respectable woman)

형님 (hyung-nim Older brother or somebody for get some kinds of credits from him)

가문 (ga-mun Status of family) =집안 (zib-an) 양반 (yang-ban Good family)=좋은 집안(zoh-eun zib-an)

평민 (pyung-min General citizen) 국민 (Kug-min Citizen = 백성 Baeg-suhng)

종 (zong Servant) 머슴 (muh-seum Housekeeper) 유모 (yu-mo infant nursing sitter)

보모 (bo-mo Babysitter)식모 (sig-mo House keeping maid)= 가정부 (Ga-zuhng-bu)

문지기 (mun-zi-gi Doorman)

No.16 The Korean Proverbs

Han-gug Sog-dam-zib 속담 (proverb)

@ 하면 된다 ha-muhn dwoen-da

If you try , you would make it.

하 (do, try = 하다) 면 (if = 그러면) 된다 (make = 되다)

@ 자기 일에 충실하라 za-gi yil-e chung-sil-ha-ra

Complete on your own job.

자기(oneself) 일(job)에(on) 충실(complete)하라(do)

@ 아는 것이 힘이다 a-neun guts-i him-i-da

The knowledge is the power

아는(to know) 것 (thing)= (앎   knowledge = 지식 zi-sig,)

앎 arm = 안다 (an-da, know 의 ('s)명사형 (noun shape)이 (s.s.)힘 (power) 이다(is)

@ 아는 길도 물어가라 a-neun gil-do mul-uh-ga-ra

Ask anyway even though you previously knew it .

아는 (used to know) 길 (way) 도 (even) 물어 (ask) 가라 (go)

@ 징검다리도 두들기며 가라   zing-zuhm-da-ri-do du-deul-gi-myuh ga-ra

Walk on the wooden bridge making sure that it is stable.

(means It is better to make sure before decide to walk on it).

징검다리 (wooden bridge)도 (even) 두들기며 (with hit) 가라 (go)

@ 인내는 쓰고 열매는 달다 in-nae-neun sseu-go yuhl-mae-neun dalda

The endurance is bitter and the fruit is sweet.

인내 (endurance) 는 (s.s) 쓰고 (bitter) 열매 (frurit) 달다 (sweet)

@　티끌 몽아 태산이다　ti-ggeul moh-a tae-san-i-da

A little saviings makes a millionaire.

티끌 (dust, a particle) 몽아(gether) 태산 (a mountain name)

@　뭉치면 살고 헤어지면 죽는다　mung-chi-myuhn sal-go he-uh-zi-myuhn zug-neun-da

If together makes the life but apart takes it away.   (This means , better to get along)

뭉치면 (together) 살고(live) 헤어지면 (apart) 죽는다 (die)

@　백짓장도 맞들면 낫다　baeg-zits-zang-do matz-deul-myuhn nats-da

It is better if hold a big paper sheet by two people.

(means, it is better help each other whatsoever)

백짓장 (a white paper sheet around one yard by two yards size) 도 (even)

맞들 (맞들다 hold by two people) 먄 (if) 낫다 (better).

@　실패는 성공의 어머니다　sil-pae-neun suhng-gong-euy uh-muh-ni-da

The failure makes the success

실패 (failure) 성공(sucess) 의 (possessive suffix) 어머니 (mother)

@　하늘이 무너져도 솟아 날 구멍이 있다

ha-neul-i mu-nuh-zyuh-do sos-a nal gu-muhng-i yits-da

There is a way to live even when the sky falls down

(means, there is a solution for any situation)

하늘 (sky) 무너져도 (fall down) 솟아 나다 (sprout) 솟아날 (for sprout)구멍(hole)

@　콩 심은 데에 콩나고 팥 심은 데에 팥 난다

kong sim-eun de-e kong-na-go pat sim-eun de pat nan-da

The bean grows where the bean was pranted, and

the red bean grows where they were pranted.

(means, everything you deserved or earned)

콩 (bean) 심은 (pranted) 데에 (at place) 콩 (bean) 나고 (sprout and)

팥(red bean) 난다(sprout)

@ 천리길도 한 걸음부터 chun-ri-gil-do han guhl-eum-bu-tuh

There is a first step to make a thousand miles (means, a start makes the success)

천 (thousand) 리 (a unit of distance, 1리 is around 0.3 miles)

길(road) 도(even, and) 한 (one) 걸음 (step) 부터 (from)

@ 참는 것이 약이다 cham-neun guhts -i jag-i-da

The patience is the medicine.

참는것 (참다, patience) 이 (s.s.) 약 (medicine) 이다 (is)

@ 올라 가지 못 할 나무는 쳐다보지도 마라

ol-ra ga-zi mots hal na-mu-neun chyuh-da-bo-zi-do ma-ra

Don't even look at the tree that you can't climb up.

올라가다 (climb) 못 할 (can't) 나무 (tree)

쳐다보다 (look at) 도 (even) 마라 (don't)

@ 좋은 약은 입에 쓰다 zoth-eun jag-eun yib-e sseu-da

Good medicine tastes bitter in the mouth.

좋은 (good) 약 (medicine) 은 (s.s.) 입 (mouth) 에 (in) 쓰다 (bitter).

@ 모르면서 아는척 마라 mo-reu-myuhn-suh a-neun-chug ma-ra

Don't pretend that you know it even though you don't know it

모르면서 (even though you don't know) 아는 (to know)척 (pretend) 마라 (don't)

@ 부엌에 칼도 안쓰면 녹난다 bu-uhk-e kal-do an-sseu-muhn nog-nan-da

A knife in the kitchen gets rusty if not used.

부엌 (kitchen) 에 (at) 칼 (knife) 도(even)

안 (doesn't) 쓰면 (use) 녹(rust) 난다 (get)

@ 남의 일에 참견마라 nam-euy yil-e cham-gyuhn-ma-ra

Don't participate in another's business

남(other)의(possesive.s.) 일(business, job)에(in)참견(participate)마라(don't)

@ 미운 사람 떡 하나 더 준다 mi-un-sa-ram dduhg ha-na duh zun-da

Give one more cookie to someone who you hate

(means people try to hide how much they hate them) .

미운 (hate) 사람 (person) 떡 (cake) 하나 (one) 더 (More) 준다 (give)

@ 양반은 물 마시고 이 쑤신다   yan-ban-eun mul na-si go yi ssu-sin-da

Good family uses the toothpick even after drinking water

(means , the good family keeps their reputation)

양반(good family)은(s.s.)물(water)마시고(drink)이(teeth)쑤신다(using tooth pick)

@ 금강산도 식후경이라 geum-gang-san-do sig-hu-gyuhng-i-ra

Keum-gang mountain trips should be done after eating.

(means, eat first, eating is important).

금강산 (a beautiful mountain in korea) 도(even, and)

식 (food, eat) 후(after) 경(sight see) 이라(is)

@ 건강이 재산이다 .guhn-gang-i zae-san-i-da

The healthy is the property.

건강 (healthy) 이 (s.s) 재산 (property) 이다 (is)

@ 황금을 보기를 돌 같이 하라 hwang-geum-eul bo-gi-reul dol gat-i ha-ra

Deal with the golds as like as the stones .

황금 (yellow gold , 금 is gold) 보기(consider, deal) 를 (with)

돌 (stone) 깉이 (as like) 하라 (do)

(means, there are more valuables then money)

@ 식은 죽 먹기다 sig-eun zug muhg-i-da

It is like eating the cold soup   (means, it is a piece of cake , it is so easy)

식은 (cold) 죽 (soup) 먹기 (to eat) 다 (is)

@ 그림의 떡이다 geu-rim-euy dduhg-i-da

The cake in the picture   (means please forget about it)

그림 (picture) 의 (possesive s.) 떡 (cake) 이다 (is)

@ 밖에서 노는 사람 밥은 있어도 자는 사람 밥은 없다

bbag-e-suh no-neun sa-ram bab-eun yitss-uh-do za-neun sa-ram bab-eun uhbs-da

There is rice for one playing outside but not for one sleeping

(means too much sleeps no food , simply lazy person no food)

밖 (out side) 에서 (at) 노는 (play) 사람 (person) 밥 (rice) 은 (s.s.)

있어도(even though there is) 자 (자다 sleep)는 (s.s.) 없다 (there isn't)

@ 소 잃고 외양간 고친다 so-ilh-go woe-yang-gan go-chin-da

Fix the cowshed after losing the cow (means too late).

소 (cow) 잃고 (lost) 외양간 (cowshed) 고친다 (fix)

@ 깨진 독에 물 붓기다 ggae-zin dog-e mul buts-gi-da

It is like pouring the water to the broken jar

(means, useless things to do , not worthy)

깨진 (broken) 독 (jar) 에 (at) 물 (water) 붓기다 (pour) .

@ 세 살 버릇 여든까지 간다 se sal buh-reuts yuh-deungga-zi gan-da

Three year old's habits can go for eighty years

세살 (three years old) 버릇 (habit) 여든 (80) 까지 (to) 간다 (go).

@ 기는 놈 위에 나는 놈 있다 gi-neun nom wi-e na-neun nom yitss-da

There are the flying ones over the creeping ones

(means, there is somebody who smarter)

기는(creeping) 놈(person whom do not respect) 위에(over) 나는(v'. 날다 flying)

@ 사람 팔자 알 수 없다 sa-ram pal-za al su uhbs-da

No one knows one's fortunes

사람 (person ,one) 팔자 (foutune)

알 (to know, original shape is 알다) 수(way) 없다 (no)

@ 길고 짧은 것은 재 봐야 안다 gil-go zzalb-eun guhts-eun zae-bwa-ya an-da

They can find out which is longer or shorter by measuring them

(means we should measure them rather then guessing)

길(v.길다, long)고 (and) 짧은 (v.짧다, short)것(thing) 은 (s.s .)

재 (v. 재다 measure) 봐야(v. 보다 see) 안다 (know , find out ,).

@ 시간이 금이다 si-gan-i geum-i-da

The time is gold.

시간 (time) 이 (s.s) 금 (gold) 이다 (is)

@ 낫 놓고 기역 자도 모른다   nats noth-go gi-yug za-do mo-reun-da

Don't know " ㄱ ' letter even though a sickle is in front of one.

(means someone has no sense at all)

낫 (sickle , just like " ㄱ " shape's the cutting grass tool)

놓고 (v. 놓다 put) 기역 (ㄱ, gi-yuhg, a consonant in Korean)

자 (letter) 도(even) 모른다(no idea)

@ 아니땐 굴뚝에 연기날까   a-ni-ddaen gul-ddug-e yuhn-gi-nal=gga

How the smoke is out even though the chimney wasn't lit.

(means every results has the reasons)

@ 닭 잡아 먹고 오리발 내놓는다   dalg zab-a muhg-go o-ri-bal nae-nonh-neun-da

Showing the duck"s foot after eating a chicken (means, someone is dishonest   )

닭(chicken) 잡아(kill)먹고(eat)오리 (duck)발(feet) 내(out)놓는다 (put, show)

@ 낮 말은 새가 듣고 밤 말은 쥐가 듣는다

natz mal-eun sae-ga deutd-go   bam mal-eun zwi-ga deutd-neun-da

The bird listens to the words in the day and the mice listen in the night

(means, Be careful what we saying).

낮 (day) 말 (saying, talk) 은(s.s.) 새 (bird) 가 (s.s.)

듣고 (listen) 고 (=그리고 and) 밤 (night) 쥐 (mice)

@ 입은 삐뚜러져도 말은 바로하라   ib-eun bbi-ddu-ruh-zyuh-do mal-eun ba-ro-ha-ra

Even lips get crooked, speak straightly

입 (mouth) 은 (s.s.) 삐뚜러져 (crooked) 도 (even)

말 (speak) 은 (s.s) 바로 (strightly) 하라 (do)

@ 이웃 사촌이라 i-uts-sa-chon-i-ra

The neighbor is the cousin . (means be nice to neighbors)

.이웃(neihgbor) 사촌 (cousin) 이라(is) =이다

@ 공든 탑이 무너지랴 gong-deun-tab-i mu-nuh-zi-rya

How can the tower fall that had the effort. (means do your best)

공든 (effort in) 탑 (tower) 이(s.s.) 무너지 (fall) 랴 (how can)

@ 꼬리가 길면 붙잡힌다   ggo-ri-ga gil-muhn but-zab-hin-da

They were caught because of it's long tail. (means nothing can not hide)

꼬리 (tail) 가 (s.s.) 길 (v.길다 long) 면 (if) 붙잡힌다 (get cut, catch).

@ 가는 사람 붙잡지 말고 오는 사람 막지마라

ga-neun-sa-ram buts-zab-zi mal-go   o-neun sa-ram mag-zi-ma-ra

Don't try holding on to someone   who would wants to go and

not away from who would wants to come   (means Let it go)

가는 (to go) 사람 (person,one) 붙잡지 (v .붙잡다 , hold)

말고 (don't) 오는 (to come)   막지 (v.막다, away, close)

@ 바람 부는대로 살아라   ba-ram bu-neun-dae-ro sal-a-ra

Live the way the winds blows. (means, no against the wind)

바람 (wind) 부는 (blow) 대로 (as) 살아라 (do live) 살다 live)

@ 뱁새가 황새 따라가면 가랭이 찌져진다

baeb-sae-ga hwoeng-sae Da-ra-ga-myuhn ga-raeng-i zzi-zuh-zin-da

The crow"s legs gets ripped up after copying the crane's steps

(means, don't copy others if you cannot afford it)

뱁새 (craw, a small bird) 가 (s.s .) 황새 (crane, a big bird)

따라 (follw) 가면 (v,가다, go) 가랭이 (leg, crotch) 찌져진다 (gets rip up)

@ 음지가 양지되고 양지가 음지된다

eum-zi-ga yang-zi-dwoe-go yang-zi-ga eum-zi dwoen-da

The shadow turns to the bright place   and the bright place turns into the shadow

(means, People's fortunes changes)

음지 (shadow place) 가 (s.s.) 양지 (bright place) 되고 (v. 되다 get)

@ 부부일심동체   bu-bu-il-sim-dong-che

The couple should have one mind and one body.

부부 (husband and wife, couple) 일 (one) 심 (mind = 마음 ma-eum)

동 (same) 체 (body =몸 mom)

@ 부부 싸음은 칼로 물베기다   bu-bu-ssa-um-eun kal-ro mul-be-gi-da

The couple argue like cutting water with a knife.

(means, Couples get along easily after argueing)

부부(couple) 싸움(argue) 은(s.s) 칼(knife)로(with)물(water) 베기다(cut).

@ 가래로 막을 것을 삽으로 막는다   ga-rae-ro mag-eul guhts-eul sab-eu-ro mag-eun-da

Using the big shovel for a thing could be prevented by a smaller one

(means,   should solve problems on time)

가래 (small shovel) 로 (with) 막을 (for prevent , objective shape of   막다)

것(thing)을(objctive s.) 삽 (shovel) 으로 (with) 막는다 (prevent), verb shape)

@ 아 소리 다르고 어 소리 다르다 ah so-ri da-reu-go uh so-ri da-reu-da

The sound " ah " different with " uh" (means, be careful how we speak).

아 (ah) 소리 (sound) 다르 (v. 다르다, different) 고 (and) 어 (uh)

@ 여자가 셋 모이면 접시가 깨진다

yuh-za-ga sets mo-i-myuhn zuhb-si-ga ggae-zin-da

The dishes get broken if three women are together. (means, women likes to talk).

여자 (woman)셋 (three) 모이(v. 모이다, together) 면 (if)

접시(dishes) 가 (s.s) 깨진다 (broken)

@ 지렁이도 밟으면 꿈쩍거린다

zi-rung-i-do balb-eu-myuhn ggum-zzuhg-guh-rin-da

The worm can move if stepped on. (means, leave them alone)

지렁이 (worm) 도 (even) 밟으면 (step) 꿈쩍거린다   move)

@ 손뼉도 마주쳐야 소리가 난다 son-bbuhg-do ma-zu-chuh-ya so-ri-ga nan-da

The clap makes the sound if the hands hit together

(means , both parts had responsibles.)

손뼉 (clap) 도(even) 마주쳐야 (hit together)소리 (sound)가 (s.s .) 난다 (out)

@ 공은 쌓은 대로 가고 죄는 지은 대로 간다

gong-eun ssath-eun dae-ro ga-go zwoe-neun zi-eun dae-ro gan-da

(The merits and sins earn.s)

공 (merit) 은(s.s.) 쌓은 (made up) 대로 (as) 가고 (go))

죄 (sin) 는 (s.s.) 지은 (make) 대로 (as) 간다 (go)

@ 웃으면 복이 온다 us-eu-myuhn bog-i-on-da

Laughs makes luck.

웃 (original shape is 웃다 means laugh)으면 (if) 복 (luck) 이 (s.s.) 온다 (come   )

No.17 The Mimesis and Onomatopoeia (의태어와 의성어)

한국인들은 의태어와 의성어를 일반적으로 사용하지만 항상 쓰지는 않는다

그렇지만, 의태어와 의성여는 말의 뜻을 강하게 표현 하여준다..

Korean use the mimesis and onomatopoeia wards in usually but not always

although, the mimesis and onomatopoeia makes strong expressions to meaning of word'.

@ 의태어 (euh-tae-uh) The Mimesis

정의 ; (zuhng-euh,) Definition

모양이나 감정을 표현하는 단어   mo-yang-i-na gam-zuhng-eul pyo-huhn-ha-neun dan-uh

The words that descrribe the shapes or emotion.

모양(shape) 이나 (or) 감정(emotion) 을 (objective.s)

표현(describe) 하는(would) 단어 (word)

깡충깡충 ggang-chung-ggang-chung

예 (ye   ex.) 토끼가 깡충깡충 뛴다.   to-ggi-ga ggang-chung-ggan-chung ddwin-da

A rabbit is gganchung ggangchung jumping.

예 ye (ex , example) 토끼 (rabbit) 가 (a sujective suffix)

깡충깡충 (a shape of run like hoping hoping)

토실토실 to-sil-to-sil

예 우리 아기가 토실토실 잘 큰다. wu-ri a-gi-ga to-sil-to-sil zal-keun-da

Our baby is tosil tosil growing well .

우리 (our) 아기(baby)가 (s.s.) 토실토실(a cute chubby look)잘 (well)큰다(grow)

복실복실 bog-sil-bog-sil

예 우리 아기는 복실복실하게 생겼어요.

wu-ri a-gi-neun big-sil-big-sil-ha-ge saeng-guhtss-uh-yo

Our baby looks bogsil bogsil.

복실복실 (seems lucky) 생겼어요 (looks)

방실방실 bang-sil-bang-sil

예 아기가 방실방실 웃는다. a-gi-ga bang-sil-bang-sil uts-neun-da

The baby is bangsil bangsil laughing.

아기 (baby) 가 (a subjective suffix) 웃는다 (laugh) 방실방실 (a lovely smile looks)

방긋방긋 bang-geuts-bang-geuts

예 한 소녀가 방긋방긋 웃는다. han so-nyh-ga bang-geuts-bang-geuts uts-neun-da

A girl is banggeuts bangbeuts laughing.

한 (one , a) 소녀 (girl) 방긋방긋 (a bright smile)

빵끗빵끗 bbang-ggeuts-bbang-ggeuts

is more stronger expressions than 방긋방긋

싱글벙글 sing-geul-buhng-geul

예 미쓰터 김이 싱글벙글 웃는다 mi-sseu-tuh kim-i sing-geul-buhng-geul uts-neun-da

Mr. Kim is singgeul buhnggeu laughing.

미쓰터 김 (Mr. Kim)   싱글벙글 (a shape of happy smiles)

생글생글 saeng-geul-saeng-geul

에 미쓰리가 생글생글거리니 좋은 일이 있나 봐

mi-sseu-ri-ga sang-geul-saeng-geul-guh-ri-ni   zoh-eun-il-i itss-na-bwa

Miss Lee might have a good thing , so she does saenggeul saenggeul

미쓰 리 (Miss Lee) 생글생글(shapes of happy smile for girl) 거리니 (doing so)

좋은 (good) 일(happening, matter, thing) 있나 (has, got) 봐 (might,　looks like)

능글능글 neung-geul-neung-geul

예 저 남자는 너무 능글능글해서 징그러워 죽겠어

zuh-nam-za-neun nuh-mu neung-geul-neung-geul-hae-suh zing-geu-ruh-wou-zug-getss-uh

That guy makes me feels creepy to dying   because of he is so neunggeul neuhggeu.l

저 (that) 남자 (guy) 너무(so, too much) 징그러워 (creepy) 죽겠어 (feel like dying)

능글능글 (a shape of stranger or funny behavior)

도리도리 do-ri-do-ri

예 우리 아기가 벌서 도리도리를 할줄 안단다.

u-ri-a-gi-ga buhl-ssuh do-ri-do-ri-reul hal-zil-an-dan-da

My baby already knows how to do doridori.

아기 (baby) 가 (a subjective s) 벌써 (already)할줄(how to do)

도리도리 (the shape of moving the head to the right and left side about the baby)

살랑살랑 sal-rang-sal-rang

예 따듯한 봄 바람이 살랑살랑 불어 온다

dda-ddeuts-han bom-ba-ram-i sal-ran-sal-ran bul-uh-on-da.

The warm spring winds breesze salrang salrang

따듯한 (warm)봄(spring) 바람(wind) 이(s.s.)

살랑살랑 (lightly) 불어(breeze) 온다(　to coming)

빈들빈들 bindeul-bindeul

예 저 남자는 왜 일 안 하고 빈들빈들 하냐 ?

zuh nam-za-neun wae il-an-ha-go bin-deul-bin-deul ha-na

Why does that man bindeul bindeul without doing any work ?

저 (that)남자 (man) 왜 (why) 일 (work) 안 (a oppositive prefix) 하고(doing)

빈들빈들 (moving around without do anything) 하냐 (do's question shape)

반짝반짝 banzzag-ban-zzag

예 샛별이 반짝반짝 빛난다

saets-buhl-i ban-zzag-banzzag bit-nan-da

.Venus shines banzzakg banzzakg

샛별(Venus) 이 (a subjective suffix) 반짝반짝 (a shape of shiny) 빛난다 (shine)

번쩍번쩍 buhn-zzuhg-buhn-zzuhg

예 그녀의 다이야몬드 반지가 번쩍번쩍 거린다.

geu-nuh-euy da-i-a-mon-deu ban-zi-ga   buhn-zzuhg-buhnzzuhg-guh-rin-da

Her diamond ring sparkles. buhnzzuhkg buhnzzuhkg.

그녀의 (her) 반지(ring) 가 (s.s.) 번쩍번쩍 (a shape of sparkling   ) 거린다 (does)

보슬보슬 boseul-boseul

예 흰 눈이 보슬보슬 내려옵니다.

heun-nun-i bo-seul-bo-seul nae-ruh-om-ni-da

The white snows boseul boseul coming down.

흰 (white) 눈(snow) 보슬보슬 (a light and soft shape) 내려옵니다 (come down)

펄펄 puhl-puhl

예 밖에는 펄펄 눈이 옵니다.

bagg-e-neun puhl-puhl nun-i omb-ni-da

Puhl puhl snowing at outside.

밖 (outside) 에는 (at,) 펄펄 (a shape of falling or moving) 눈이 옵니다 (snowing)

팔딱파딱 pal-ddag-pal-ddag

예 갓 잡아온 생선이 바구니에서 팔딱팔딱 뜁니다

gats zab-a-on saeng-suhn-i ba-gu-ni-e-suh pal-ddag-pal-ddag ddwim-ni-da.

They just caught fish palddakg palddakg jumps in the basket..

갓 (just) 잡아온 (catched) 생선 (fish) 바구니 (basket) 에서 (in), 뜁니다(jump)

팔딱팔딱 (a shape of jump = 펄떡퍼떡 puhldduhkg-puhldduhkg)

펄럭펄럭 puhl-ruhg-puhl-ruhg

예 깃발이 펄럭펄럭 바람에 춤을 춥니다.

gits-bal-i puhl-ruhg- puhl-ruhg ba-ram-e chum-eul chumb-ni-da

The flag is puhlrukg puhlrukg dancing in the wind.

깃발 (flag) 펄럭(a shape of moving = 팔락팔락 palrakg)   이 (s.s.)

바람 (wind) 에(by) 춤 (dance) 을 (a objective s.) 춥니다 (dance)

헐떡헐떡 hul-dduhd-hul-dduhg

예 날씨가 너무 더워서 모두들 헐떡헐떡 합니다

nal-ssi-ga nuh-mu duh-wou-suh mo-du-deul huhl-dduhg-huhl-dduhg hamb-ni-da

The weather is too hot , everybody does huldukg-huldukg.

헐떡헐떡 (means getting short of breath or thirsty = 할딱하딱 halddag-halddag)

날씨(weather) 너무(too) 더워 (hot) 모두 (every) 들 (pulal suffix)거립니다 (does)

옹기종기 ong-gi-jong-gi

예 그의 친척들이 이 동네에서 옹기종기 모여 삽니다.

geu-euy chin-chug-deul-i yi dong-ne-e-suh   ong-gi-zong-gi mo-yuh sab-ni-da

His relation ongi jongi living at this neighbor.

옹기종기 (means looks close and friendly)그의 (his) 친척들(relations) 이 (s.s.)

이 (this, when 이 comes front of word) 동네 (town) 모여 (together) 삽니다 (living)

아기자기 a-gi-za-gi

예 그들은 결혼하여 아기자기 잘 살고있다

geu-deul-eun gyuhl-hon-ha-yuh a-gi-za-gi zal-sal-go-itss-da

They married and agizagi living well.

아기자기 (means same as 오손도손 oson-doson which is looks so happy and fun)

그들 (they) 결혼 (marrige) 하여(did) 잘 (well) 살고있다 (living)

왔다갔다 watss-da-gatss-da

예 영수야 왔다갔다 하지말고 앉아라.

yuhng-su-ya watss-da-gatss-da ha-zi-mal-go anz-a-ra

Yuhngsu please sit down without watsda gatsda.

왔다갔다 (means   coming and going that makes others dizzy or confused   )

영수 (Yuhngsu) 야 (a calling suffix)

P.s. Koreans put " 아 or 야 "after name when they call someone younger or friend.

왔다 (come) 갔다 (gone) 하지말고 (without do) 앉아라 (sit down)

왔다리갔다리 watss-da-ri-gatss-da-ri is same means as 왔다갔다

갈팡질팡 gal-pang-zil-pang

예 그는 술이 취해서 갈팡질팡 거린다.

geu-neun sul-i chi-hae-suh gal-pang-zil-pang guh-rin-da

He is galpang zilpang from drunkness.

그는 (he) 술이취해서 (got drunk) 거린다 (does)

갈팡질팡 (taking this way or that way instead of straightly)

싱숭생숭 sing-sung-saeng-sung

예 나는 내 마음이 싱숭생숭해서 차라리 잠을 잤다.

na-neun ma-eum-i sing-sung-saeng-sunghae-suh cha-ra-ri zam-eul zatss-da

I would rather sleep because my mind is singsung saengsung.

싱숭생숭 (a kind of confusing) 나는 (I) 내 (my) 마음(mind)

차라리 (rather) 잠을잤다(take a sleep)

생생 saeng-saeng

예 잠을 잘 자고나니 내기분이 생생해졌다

zam-eul zal za-go-na-ni nae gi-bun-i saeng-saeng-hae-zyuhtss-da.

After sleeping , my feelings are saeng saeng.

잠 (sleep) 잘 (well) 자고나니(after slept) 내 (= 나의 my)

기분 (feeling , mood) 이(s.s.) 생생하다 (clear, flashness)

본듯만듯 bon-deuts-man-deuts

예 그가 너에게 오면 절대로 본듯만듯 하지마라.

geu-ga nuh-e-ge o-muhn zuhl-cae-ro bon-deuts man-deuts ha-zi-ma-ra

If he comes to you, never do bondeuts mandeuts.

본듯만듯 (looks like seen or not , means not interesting)그가 (he)너에게 (to you) 오면 (if come) 절대로 (never) 본듯(like see) 만듯 (didn't see)하지마라 (don't do)

할까말까 hal-gga-mal-gga

예 그는 아직도 그 일을 할까말까 망설이고 있다

geu-neun a-zig-do geu il-eul hal-gga-mal-gga mang-suhl-i-go itss-da.

He is still hesitating for that matter to halgga malgga.

아직도 (still) 그 (that) 일 (job. matter) 할까말까 (do or not do)

망설이고 (hesitate) 있다 (is)

안절부절 an-zuhl-bu-zuhl

예 그는 시험에 합격이 되어 좋아서 안접부절 못 하고있다

geu-neun si-huhm-e hab-guhg-i-dwoe-uh zoh-a-suh

an-zuhl-bu-zuhl mots-ha-go-itss-da

He couldn't anzuhl-buzuhl because he was happy that he passed the test.

시험 (test, examination) 합격 (passed) 되다 (made) 좋아서 (happy, delight)

안절부절 (don't know what to do) 못 (can't) 하고있다 (does)

꾸물꾸물 ggu-mul-ggu-mul

예 영식아, 꾸물꾸물 하지말고 빨리 와라

yuhng-sig-a ggu-mul-ggu-mul-ha-zi-mal-go bbal-ei-wa-ra.

Yuhng-sig , hurry come without ggumul-ggumul.

영식 (Yuhng-sig) 아 (a calling name suffix) 꾸물꾸물 (slowly, taking time)

하지말고 (don't) 빨리 (hurry) 와라 (come , get here)

어정청 uh-zuhng-chuhng

예 자네 어정청 섯지 말고 여기 앉으시오.

za-ne uh-zuhng-chuhng suhts-zi-mal-go yuh-gi-anz-eu-si-o

Dear you please sit here without uhzuhngchung standing up.

자네 (you, dear you,) 어정청(looks guppy) 섯지 (stand up)

말고 (without, don't) 여기 (here) 앉으시오(please sit down)

가물가물 ga-mul-ga-mul

예 안개가 껴서 앞이 가물가물거린다.

an-gae-ga gguh-suh ap-i ga-mul-ga-mul-guh-rin-da

The fog makes gamul gamul in front.

안개 (fog) 가 (s.s..) 껴서 (contained) 앞 (front, sight) 이 (s.s.)

가물가물 (not clear) 거린다(make)

찬찬 chan-chan

예 그 여자는 찬찬해서 그일을 잘 할거야

geu-yuh-za-neun chan-chan-hae-suh geu il-eul zal hal-guh-ya

She will do that job well because she is chanchan.

그 여자 (She) 찬찬해서(detail)그일 (that job)을(o.s.) 잘(well) 할거야 (will do)

찰찰 chal-chal

예 내가 좋은 회사에 취직이 됐으니 우리는 찰찰히 살 수 있어요

nae-ga zoh-eun hwoe-sa-e chwi-zig-i dwoetss-eu-ni

wu-ri-neun chal-chal-hi sal-su itss-uh-yo.

We will chalchalhi live well because I was hired in a good company.

내가 (I) 좋은 (good) 회사 (company) 에 (at) 취직 (hire) 됐으니 (get)

우리 (we)는 (s.s.) 찰찰히 (enoughly) 살 (살다 live) 수 (to, the way) 있어요 (would)

창창 chang-chang

예 당신은 아직도 앞 길이 창창한 젊은 사람이야

dang-sin-eun a-zig-do ap-gil-i chang-chang-hjan zuhrm-eum sa-ram-i-ya.

You are still a young person in changchanghan coming days

당신 (you) 은 (s.s.) 아직도 (still) 앞 (coming, future)

길 (way, days in this sentence) 이 (s.s.) 창창한 (in future) 사람 (person) 이야 (are)

빽빽 bbaeg-bbaeg

예 숲 속에는 소나무들이 빽빽이 있다

sup-sog-e-neun so-na-mu-deul-i bbaeg-bbaeg-i itss-da.

The pine trees are in the forest with bbaeg bbaeg.

숲 (forest) 속에는 (in) 소나무 (pine tree) 들 (plural suffix) 이 (s.s.)

빽빽이 (very crowd) 있다 (are)

아른아른 areun-areun

예 아직도 너의 모습이 내 눈에 아른아른 거린다

a-zig-do nuh-euy mo-seub-i nae-nun-e a-reun-a-reun guh-rin-da.

Still, your image is in my eye with areunareun.

아직도 (still) 너의 (your) 모습 (image, picture, shape) 내 (my) 눈 (eye) 에 (in)

아른아른 (slightly appear, show) 거린다 (is, doing)

아리까리 ari-ggari

예 그 일은 너무 오래되어 아리까리 하다

geu il-eun nuh-mu o-rae-dwoe-uh a-ri-gga-ri ha-da.

That happened a long time ago so makes it ariggari.

그 (that) 일(matter) 은(s.s.) 너무 (too) 오래되어 (long ago)

아리까리 (not very remember) 하다 (,does)

이만저만 i-man-zuh-man

예 저 사람은 이만저만한 사람이 아니래

zuh-sa-ram-eun i-man-zuh-man-han sa-ram-i a-ni-rae.

That man is not a imanzuhman person. (not ordinary person , very great person)

저 (that) 사람 (man, person) 은 (ss..) 이만저만한 (usual   )

사람 (person) 이(a indicative suffix) 아니래(a deniable suffix, not   )

징글징글 zing-geul-zing-geul

예 뱀은 징글징글하게 생겼다

baem-eun zing-geul-zing-geul-ha-ge saeng-guhtss-da.

The snake looks zinggeulzingeul.

뱀 (snake)은(a subjecive suffix) 징글징글 (creepy) 하게 (.like) 생겼다 (looks)

주섬주섬 zu-suhm-zu-suhm

예 예들아, 방 좀 주섬주섬 치워라

ye-deul-a bang-zom zu-suhm-zu-suhm chi-wou-ra.

You kids please   zusuhm zusuhm clean up the room.

예들 (kids) 아 (a calling s.) 방(room) 좀 (please)

주섬주섬 (a shape of picking up) 치워라 (clean up)

오르락내리락 o-ri-rag-nae-ri-rag

에 이 층계는 사람들이 너무 오르락내리락 해서 벌써 망가졌어요

yi cheung-gye-neun sa-ram-deul-i nuh-mu o-reu-rag-nae-ri-rag-hae-suh

buhl-ssuh mang-ga-zuhtss-uh-yo.

These stairs are broken by being used too many people oreuragnaerirag.

이 (this) 층계 (stairs) 는 (s.s.) 사람들 (people) 이 (indicating s.) 너무 (too)

오르락내리락 (ups and downs) 해서 (did) 벌써 (already) 망가졌어요 (broken)

왁자지껄 wag-za-zi-gguhl

에 저 애들이 왜 왁자지껄 떠드는지 모르겠네.

zuh-ae-deul-i wae wag-za-zi-gguhl dduh-deu-neun-zi mo-reu-getss-ne

Wondering why those kids are making the wagza zigguhl noises.

저 (those) 애들 (kids) 이 (a indicating s.) 왜 (why) 왁자지껄 (making all sounds)

떠드는지 (noisy) 모르겠네 (don't know, wonder)

사뿐사뿐 sa-bbun-sa-bbun

에 그녀는 사뿐사뿐 예쁘게 춤춘다.

geu-nuh-neun sa-bbeun-sa-bbeun ye-bbeu-ghe chum-chun-da.

She is dancing sabbeun sabbeun prettily.

그녀 (She) 는 (s.s.) 사뿐사뿐 (lightly) 예쁘게 (lovely, prettily) 춤춘다 (dance)

덩실덩실 duhng-sil-duhng-sil   예 그도 신이나서 덩실덩실 춤춘다

geu-do sin-i-na-suh duhng-sil-duhng-sil chum-chun-da.

And he is duhngsil duhngsil dancing with joy.

그 (he) 도 (and) 신이나서 (with joy) 덩실덩실 (wider, bigger steps dance style)

@ 의성어　(euy-shng-uh) The Onomatopoeia

정의 (zuhng-euh) Definition

소리를 표현하는 단어　so-ri-reul pyo-huhn-ha-neun dan-uh

The words that would describes the sounds.

소리(sounds) 를(a objective suffix) 표현하는 (describe) 단어 (word)

짹짹　zzaeg-zaeg

ex 봄이 되니 참새가 짹짹 거린다.

bom-i-dwoe-ni cham-sae-ga zzaeg-zzaeg-guh-rin-da

The sparrows make sounds zzaeg zzaeg because the spring is here.

봄 (spring) 이 (a indicating s.) 되니 (because is)참새 (sparrow) 들(pulural s.)

이 (s.s.) 짹짹 (the kind of bird sounds) 거린다 (does , making)

멍멍　muhng-muhng

ex 저 개가 멍멍 짖으니 주인이 오나보다

zuh-gae-ga muhng-muhng zitz-eu-mi zu-in-i o-na-bo-da.

It seems like his master is coming so the dog is muhng muhng barking.

저 (that) 개(dog) 가(s.s.) 멍멍 (dog's barking　sound) 짖으(bark) 니 (so that)

주인 (master, owner) 이 (a definitive suffix) 오나 (come) 보다(seems)

야옹야옹　ya-ong-ya-ong

ex 고양이가 야옹야옹 운다. go-yang-i-ga ya-ong-ya-ong un-da

The cat is crying yaong yaong.

고양이 (cat) 가 (s.s.) 야옹야옹 (the sounds of　the cat) 운다(cry)

어흥어흥 uh-geung-uh-heung

ex 내가 동물원에 갔더니, 호랑이가 어흥어흥 거렸다

nae-ga dong-mul-woun-e gatss-duh-ni ho-rang-i-ga

uh-heung-uh-heung guh-ryuhtss-da.

When I went to the zoo, the tiger made uhheung uhheung sounds.

내가 (I) 동물원 (zoo) 에 (a locative suffix) 갔더니 (went)

호랑이 (tiger)가 (s.s.)어흥어흥 (tiger's roaring sound) 거렸다 (does)

꽥꽥 ggwaeg ggwaeg

ex 그는 무엇을 잘못 먹어서 꽥꽥 다 토해 냈다

geu-neun mu-uhtss-eul zal-mots muhg-uh-suh ggaeg-ggaeg. da to-hae-naetss-da

He ate something that was bad ggwaeg ggwaeg so he vomited it all out.

그 (he) 는 (s.s.) 무엇을 (something) 잘못(wrong) 먹어서 (ate)

꽥꽥 (not pleasant sounds) 다 (all) 토해 (vomited) 냈다 (out)

꿀꿀 ggul-ggul

ex 이 돼지는 하루종일 꿀꿀거리며 먹고있다

yi dwae-zi-neun ha-ru-zong-il ggul-ggulguh-ri-muh muhg-go-itss-da.

This pig ggul ggul eating all day long.

이 (this) 돼지 (pig) 는 (s.s.) 하루종일 (all day long)

꿀꿀 (a shape of sound) 거리며 (with) 먹고있다 (eating)

탕탕 tang-tang

ex 갑자기 탕탕 총 소리가 들여 모두 달아났다.

gab-za-gi chong so-ri-ga deul-yuh mo-du dal-a-natss-da

Suddenly everybody ran away after they heard the tang tang gun sounds

갑자기 (suddenly) 탕탕 (a shape of sounds) 총 (gun) 소리 (sound)가(indicative s.)

들여 (getting heard) 모두(everybody) 달아났다 (ran away).

빡빡 bbag-bbag

ex 내 등허리 좀 빡빡 긁어라.

nae deung-huh-ri zom bbag-bbag geulrg-uh-ra

Please bbag bbag scratch my back.

내 (= 나의 my) 등허리 (back, near waist) 좀 (please)

빡빡 (sounds like bbag-bbag) 긁어라 (do scratch)

콸콸 kwal-kwal

ex 나이아가라 폭포는 항상 콸콸 물 내려오는 소리를 낸다

na-i-a-ga-ra pog-po-neun hang-sang kwal-kwal

mul nae-ryuh-o-neun so-ri-reul naen-da.

Niagara Falls made the kwal kwal waterfall sounds all the time.

나이아가라 (Niagara) 폭포 (fall) 는 (s.s.) 항상 (all the time)

콸콸 (big water running sounds) 물 (water) 내려오는(fall down)

소리 (sounds) 를 (objective s.) 낸다 (out , give)

음메에 eum-me-e

ex 송아지가 음메에 엄마를 찾고있다

song-a-zi-ga eum-me-e uhm-ma-reul chtss-go-itss-da.

A calf eummee looking for her mom.

송아지(calf) 가 (s.s.) 음메에 (cow's cry sounds)

엄마 (mom) 를(a objective s.) 찾고 있다 (looking for)

찌르륵찌르륵 zzi-reu-reug-zzi-reu-reug

ex 어디에서 찌르륵찌르륵 소리가 나느냐 ?

uh-di-e-suh zzi-reu-reug-zzi-reu-reug so-ri-ga na-neu-nya

Where are the zzireureug zzireureug sounds coming from ?

어디 (where) 에서(from) 찌르륵 찌르륵 (the sounds like zzireureug zzireureug)

소리 (sound) 가 (s.s.) 나느냐 (made out , came out)

찍찍 zzig-zzig

ex 쥐들이 창고에서 찍찍거린다

zwi-deul-i chang-go-e-suh zzig-zzig-guh-rin-da.

The mice make zzig zzig sounds in the warehouse.

쥐들 (mices) 이 (s.s.) 창고 (warehouse) 에서(a locative s.)

찍직 (mouse's sound like zzigzzig) 거린다 (doing)

쓰르륵쓰르륵 sseu-reu-reug sseu-reu-eug

ex 쓰르라미가 쓰르륵쓰르륵 노래하니 여름이 한창 이다.

sseu-reu-ra-mi-ga seu-reu-reug-seu-reu-reug no-rae-ha-ni

yuh-eum-i-han-chang-i-da

The cicadas sseureueurg sseureureug singing sounds tells it is mid summer.

쓰르라미 (cicada) 가 (s.s .)쓰르륵 쓰르륵 (cicade's sounds) 노래 (sing)

하니(니까 , so that)여름 (summer)이 (s.s.) 한창 (mid , peak)이다 (is)

윙윙 wing-wing

ex 벌들이 꽃 주변에서 윙윙 날고있다.

buhl-deul-i ggotss zu-byuhn-e-suh wing-wing nal0go-itss-da

The bees wing wing flying around the flowers.

벌 (bee) 들(plural suffix)이 (s.s.) 꽃 (flower)주변 (around)에서 (locative s.)

윙윙 (a sound like bee's flying) 날고있다 (fly)

졸졸 zol-zol

ex 시냇물이 졸졸 흐른다. si-naets-mul-i zol-zol- heu-reun-da

A stream is zol zol flowing.

시냇물 (stream) 이 (s.s.) 졸졸(sounds of water down)흐른다 (flow)

질펀질펀 zil-puhn-zil-puhn

ex 비가 와서 땅이 질펀질펀하다.

bi-ga-wa-suh ddan-i zil-puhn-zil-puh ha-da

The ground is zilpuhn-zilpuhn after rain.

비 (rain) 가 (s's.) 와서 (because of came)땅 (groud) 이 (s.s) 질펀하다

질팡질팡 zil-pang-zil-pang is same means as 질판질펀

축축 chug-chug

ex. 아기가 물을 쏟아서 이불이 축축하다

a-gi-ga mul-eul ssotd-a-suh i-bul-i chug-chug-ha-da

The blankets got chug-chug because the baby spilled the water.

아기(baby) 가 (s.s.) 물(water) 을(o.s.) 쏟아서 (쏟다 spell + ..서 because of)

이불 (blanket) 이 (s.s.) 축축하다 (wet   )

딸그닥딸그닥 ddal-geu-dag-ddal-geu-dag

ex 부엌에서 누가 딸그닥딸그닥 하느냐?

bu-uhk-e-suh nu-ga ddal-geu-dag-ddal-geu-dag ha-neu-nya

Who goes ddalgeudag-ddalgeudag in the kitchen ?

부엌 (kitchen) 에서 (in) 누가(who) 딸그닥딸그닥 (a noisy sound) 하느냐 (does)

소근소근 so-geun-so-geun

ex 그들은 소근소근 사랑을 밤새도록 속삭였다.

geu-deul-eun so-geun-so-geun sa-rang-eul bam-sae-do-rog sog-sag-yuhtss-da

They whispered love sogeun-sogeun all night long.

그들 (they) 은 (s.s.) 소근소근 (shape of very soft sounds)

사랑 (love) 을 (o.s.) 밤새도록 (all night long) 속삭였다 (whisperd).

싹싹 ssag-ssag

ex 1 의태어 , with   Mimesis Shape

그녀는 참 싹싹한 여자다

geu-nyuh-neun chm ssag-ssag-han yuh-za-da

She is a very pleasant lady.

.   그녀 (she) 는(s.s.) 참 (very) 싹싹한 (pleasant, sociable) 여자 (woman)

ex. 2, 의성어 , With Onomatopoeia Shape

아들은 아버지께 잘못을 싹싹 빌었다

a-deul-eun a-buh-zi-gge zal-mots-eul ssag-ssag bil-uhtss-da

The son ssag-ssag asked for forgiveness from his father.

아들 (son) 은 (s.s) 아버지 (father) 께 (to; honorific word of 에게)

(p.s. honorific word = 높힘말 nop-him-mal = 존대말 zon-dae-mal)

잘못(fault) 을(o.s.) 싹싹 (a sounds with two palms massaging)

빌었다 (ask for forgiveness)

딩동딩동 ding-dong-ding-dong

ex. 누군가가 문종을 딩동딩동 누르고있다

nu-gun-ga-ga mun-zong-eul nu-reu-go itss-da

Somebody is dingdong-dingdong pushing the door bell.

누군가 (somebody) 가(s.s.) 문(door) 종(bell) 을 (o.s.)

딩동딩동 (a shape of sound) 누르고 (push' press) 있다 (is)

랄라랄라 ral-ra-ral-ra

ex. 아이들은 즐거웁게 노래를 랄라랄라 부른다

a-i-deul-eun zeul-guh-wub-ge no-rae-reul ral-ra-ral-ra bu-reun-da

The children singing songs ralr-ra-ral-ra joyfully.

아이들 (chilldren , 아이 child) 은 (s s.) 즐거웁게 (joyfully)

노래 (song) 를 (o.s) 랄라랄라 (a shape of sound) 부른다 (sing)

No.18 Korean Simple Vocabulary List (간단한 한굴 단어집)

@ 가정 (ga-zuhng   Family)

어머니 (uh-muh-ni Mother) 아버지 (a-buh-zi Father)

엄마 (uhm-ma Mom) 아빠 (a-bba   Daddy   )

할머니 (hal-muh-ni   Grandmother) 할아버지 (hal-a-buh-zi Grandfather)

형제(huhng-ze   Brothers) 자매 (za-mae Sisters)   언니 (uhn-ni Older Sister)

오빠 (o-bba Older Brother) 동생 (dong-saeng   Younger than me)

여동생 (yuh-dong-saeng   Younger sister) 남동생 (nam-dong-saeng Younger brother)

자녀 (za-nyuh Children, Kids= 자식 za-sig = 아이들 a-i-deul)

아들 (a-deul   Son) 딸 (ddal   Daughter)

손자 (son-za   Grandson) 손녀 (son-nuh Granddaughter)

증손자 (zeung-son-za Great grandson) 증손녀 (zeung-son-nyuh Great granddaughter)

@ 교육 (gyo-yug   Education)

학교 (hag-gyo   School) 공부 (gong-bu Study) 배우다 (bae-u-da   Learn)

학생 (hag-saeng   Student) 선생님 (suhn-saeng-nim Teacher) 교수 (gyo-su   Professor) 교장 (gyo-zang Principal)교감 (gyo-gam Vice Principal)

유치원 (yu-chi-woun Pre School, Kindergarten)

초등학교 (cho-deung-hag-gyo Elementary School = 국민학교   )

중학교 (zung-hag-gyo Middle School) 고등학교 (go-deung-hag-gyo High School)

전문학교 (zuhn-mun-hag-gyo Community College)

초급대학 (cho-geub-dae-hag Junior College) 대학교 (dae-hag-gyo College)

종합대학 (zong-hab-dae-hag University) 대학원 (dae-hag-woun After College)

의대 (euh-dae   Medical, or Medicine College = 의과대학)

(대 dae = 대학 dae hag = College) 학위 (hag-wi Degree)

학사 (hag-sa Bachelor) 석사 (sug-sa   Master) 박사 (bag-sa Doctor, Ph.)

상대 (sang-dae Bussiness College or School=상업대학)

공대 (gong-dae   Enginieering College = 공과대학)

약대 (yag-dae   Pharmarcy College = 약학대학) 법대 (buhb-dae Law College=법학대학)

음대 (eum-dae   Music College = 음악대학) 미대 (mi-dae   Art College = 미술대학)

인문(in-mun Humanity)체육(che-yug Physical, Athletics) 역사 (yug-sa Historic)

문리(mun-ri Liberal Arts) 과학 (gwa-hag   Science)우주(wu-zu Space, Astronaut)

지리 (zi-ri   Geography)화학(hwa-hag   Chemistry) 수학 (su-hag   Mathematics)

경제 (gyuhng-ze Economics) 경영(gyhng-yuhng Management)회계 (hwoe-gye Account)

철학 (chul-hag   Psychology) 정치(zuhng-chi Politics) 사회 (sa-hwoe Social)

무용(mu-yong Dance) 전기 (zuhn-gi Electric) 전자 (zuhn-za Electron)

기술 (gi-sul Technic, Skill) 등록(deung-rog Registration) 입학 (ib-hag Admission, enter) 학비 (hag-bi Tuition) 학점 (hag-zuhm Credit. Grade Point) 졸업(zol-uhb   Graduation)

축하(chug-ha Congratulations) 취직(chwi-zig Job Hired) 근무 (geun-mu Work,do duty) 봉사 (bong-sa Service) 봉급 (bong-geub Wage, Salary) 저금(zuh-geum Saving)

연애 (yuhn-ae Date) 결혼 (gyuhl-hon Marriage) 사랑 (sa-rang Love)

@ 사회 (sa-hwoe Social)   생활 (saeng-hwal Life)

나 (na , I) 나의 (na-euh   My) 나의 것 (na-euy-guhts Mine) 자신 (za-sin   Self)

당신 (dang-sin You) 당신의 (dang-sin-euy Your) 당신의 것 (dang-sin-euy guhts Yours)

당신자신 (za-sin Yoirself) 이웃 (i-uts Neighborhood = 동네 dong-ne)

이웃사람 (i-uts-sa-ram   Neighbor) 예의 (ye-euh   Manners) 아이 (a-i Child)

아이들 (a-i-deul Children) 어른 (uh-reun Adult) 친구(chin-gu   Friend)

친척 (chin-chuhg Relations) 방문 (bang-mun Visit) 안부 (an-bu Greetings)

편지 (pyuhn-zi Letter) 연락 (yuhn-rag Conection) 소식(so-sig News)

전화 (zuhn-hwa Call) 전화기 (zuhn-hwa-gi Telephone , Phone) 간단 (gan-dan Simple)

도덕관 (do-duhg-gwuan   Morality) 질서 (zil-suh   Order) 법 (buhb Law)

준수 (zun-su Keep = 지키다) 안전 (an-zuhn safe) 건물 (guhn-mul Buildings)

시설(si-suhl   Faciliies) 애용 (ae-yong   Using always cautiously)

상호 (sang-ho Eachother)   햅조 (huhb-zo Coperate , Help) 단결 (dan-gyuhl Unify)

환경 (hwan-gyuhng Environmental) 관리(gwan-ri Manager) 미화 (mi-hwa   Beutify)

자연(za-yuhn   Nature)보호(bo-ho Protect) 도시(do-si City) 시청 (si-chuhng   City Hall)

시장(si-zang Mayor)사무실 (sa-mu-sil Office) 사무원 (sa-mu-woun Office Worker)

@ 정부 (zuhng-bu Government)

대통령 (dae-tong-ryuhng President) 부통령 (bu-tong-ryuhng Vice President)

국회 (gug-hwoe Congress)국화의원(gug-hwoe-euy-won Senate)선거 (suhn-guh Election)공화당 (gong-hwa-dang Republic) 민주당 (min-zu-dang Democrat)

여당 (yuh-dang Government Party) 야당 (ya-dang Opposite Party)

대사관 (dae-sa-gwan   Ambassador) 관청 (gwan-chuhng   Government Offices)

회사 (hwoe-sa   Company) 공무원 (gong-mu-woun Government Officers)

장관 (zang-gwan Cabinet Minister) 문교부 (mun-gyo-bu   Educational Administritons)

보건사회부 (bo-guhn-sa-hwoe-bu Health and Society Adm.)

상공부 (sang-gong-bu   Trade and Industry Administratios)무역 (mu-yuhg Trade)

거래 (guh-rae Deal) 국방부 (gug-bang-bu   National Defense   Administrations Military)

육군 (yug-gun   Army) 공군 (gong-gun   Air force) 해군 (hae-gun   Navy)

해병대 (hae-byuhng-dae   Marine)   군인 (gun-in   Soldier)   대장 (dae-zang Generals)

농림부 (nong-rim-bu   Agriculture   Administrations)씨 (ssi Sead) 뿌리(bbu-ri   Root)

곡물 (gog-mul Grains) 과일(gwa-il Fruit) 야채 (ya-chae Vegetables=채소chae-so)

식물 (sig-mul Plant) 나무 (na-mu Tree) 밭 (bat   Field ,Farm)열매 (yuhl-mae Fruit)

뿌리(bbu-ri Root) 버섯 (buh-suhts Mushroom) 꽃 (ggoth flower)

재배 (ze-bae   Caltivation , Growing = 경작 gyuhng-zag)

농산물 (nong-san-mul Farm Products) 수확 (su-hwag Harvesting)

풍년(pung-nyuhn Good harvest year) 흉년 (hyung-nyuhn Bad harvest year)

@ 직장 (zig-zang   Work Place,   Employer)

회사 (hwoe-sa Company) 사장 (sa-zang   Chief, President)

부사장 (bu-sa-zang Vice president) 회장 (hwoe-zang Chairman)

면접 (myuhn-zuhb Interview) 추천 (chu-chun Recomendation) 안내 (an-ne Guide)

소개 (so-gae Introduce) 총무 (chong-mu   Director)

인사부 (in-sa-bu   Manage employee and humanity Department)

기획부 (gi-hwoeg-bu Planning Department)

사무부 (sa-mu-bu Paper Work Department)

영업부 (yuhng-uhb-bu Business Department) 재정 (zae-zuhng   Financial)

실험실(sil-huhm-sil Laboratory) 편집 (pyuhn-zib   Edit) 광고 (gwang-go Advertise)

판매 (pan-mae Sale) 보고(bo-go Report)계산 (gye-san Calcurate) 장부(zang-bu Book)

행정관리(haeng-zuhng-gwan-ri Management, Administration)

현지답사 (hyuhn-zi-dab-sa Survey) 감사 (gam-sa Investigation = 조사 zo-sa)

p.s. 감사합니다 gam-sa-ham-ni-da means Thank you .

Some Korean words have multi differant meanings

Ex 가 (ga means Go , Music , Edge, Price, Yes, Grade F, Last Name,

Family. House, Street , Laugh loudly, Addition, Not Real)

한국어는 순수한 한국어와 중국어에서 유래한 한자어가있다.

han-gug-uh-neun sun-su-han han-gug-uh-wa zung-gug-uh-e-suh yu-rae-han han-za-uh-ga-itss-da

The Korean has the pure korean words and the HanZaUh which originated from the Chinese caracters.

한국어 (han-gug-uh Korea's Language = 한국말 han-gug-mal)

은(a subjective suffix , other means Silver) 순수한 (sun-su-han Pure)

한국어(korean) 와(wa And) 중국어(zung-gug-uh Chinese) 에서 (e-suh From)

유래한 (yu-rae-han Originated) 한자어 (ha-za-uh Hanza)가 (s.s) 있다 (itss-da   has, are)

기록 (gi-rog Record) 운영 (un-yuhng Operate)공장 (gong-zang Productions plant)

공장장 (gong-zang-zang   Superintendant , Plant Chairman) 비서(bi-suh Secretary)

상사 (sang-sa Boss)직원 (zig-woun Employee) 동료 (dong-ryo Fellow)

청소부 (chuhng-so-bu Jenitor) 문지기(mun-zi-gi Doorman)

경비원(gyuhng-bi-woun Security Guard man)

@ 도서관 (do-suh-gwan Library)

열남실 (yuhl-nam-sil Reading Room) 도서목록 (do-suh-mog-rog   Book List)

책 (chaeg Book= 도서) 책빌림 (chaeg-bil-rim Land Books) 반납(ban-nap   Return)

컴퓨터실 (kom-pyu-tuh-sil Computer Room)책상(chaeg-sang Table, Desk)

의자 (euy-za Chair)휴계실 (hyu=gye-sil Relaxing Room , Intermission Room)

@ 은행 (eun-haeng Bank)

돈 (don Money) 화폐 (hwa-pye Currency)금융 (geum-yung Circulation of Money)

금융시장 (geum-yung-si-zang, Money Market) 융자 (yung-za Financing)

이자 (i-za Interest) 단리(dan-ri Simple interest) 복리 (bog-ri Copound Interest)

무이자 (mu-i-za No Interest) 원금(woun-geum Principal, Capital)

지불 (zi-bul Payment) 상환(sang-hwhn Exchange)기한(간) (gi-han(gan) Length, term)

수입 (su-ib Income) 년수입 (nuhn-su-ib Annual Income)봉급(bong-geub Wage, Income)

일급 (il-geub Daily Wage) 주급 (zu-geub Weekly Wage)

월급 (woul-geub Monthly Wage Salary) 년금(nyuhn-geum Yearly Wage)

상여금 (sang-yuh-geum Bonus = 특별수당 teug-byuhl-su-dang)

보상금 (bo-sang-geum Compensation) 지불 (zi-bul Payment)잔돈(zan-don Change)

입금 (ib-geun Deposit) 회수금 (hwoe-su-geum Withdraw) 잔금 (zan-geum Balance)

송금 (song-geum Transfer , Sending money) 영수증 (yuhng-su-zeung Receipts)

저금 (zuh-geum Saving = 예금 ye-geum) 지출(zi-chul Spend, Expend , Disbursment)

잔고 (zan-go Balance) 통장(tong-zang Bank book) 개인 (gae-in Personal)

이름 (i-reum Name) 구좌번호 (gu-zwa Account Number)

신용카드 (sin-yong-ka-deu Credit Card) 암호 (am-ho Password)

@ 무역 (mu-yuhg Trade) 사업 (sa-uhb Business)

연구 (yuhn-gu Study) 발명(bal-myuhng Invention) 특허 (teug-huh Patent Right)

계획(gye-hwoeg Plan) 자본 (za-bon Fund, Capital) 투자 (tu-za Investment)

원료 (won-ryo Raw Material) 구입 (gu-ib Purchase Buy) 구매 (gu-mae = 구입)

제조 (ze-zo Making Producing) 제품 (ze-pum Production)

광고 (gwang-go Advertisement) 수출 (su-chul Export) 수입 (su-ib Import)

판매 (pan-mae Sale) 매상 (mae-sang Sales) 불량품(bul-ryang-pum Bad Product)

반납 (ban-nab Return) 재고(zae-go Stock) 보상 (bo-sang Recover) 소비(so-bi Spend)

이익(i-ig Gain profit) 손해 (son-hae Damage) 적자 (zuhg-za   Loss)

흑자 (heug-za Gain) 인기 (in-gi Popular) 주문(zu-mun Order) 시장 (si-zang Market)

매진 (mae-zin Selling out , Out of stock) 상인(sang-in Merchant)

시장조사 (si-zang-zo-sa   Market Survey) 경쟁 (gyuhng-zaeng Competition)

견본(gyuhn-bon Sample) 인력 (in-ryuhg   Human Power , Man Made)

인건비 (in-guhn-bi   Labor Costs) 동력 (dong-ryuhg Power) 직원 (zig-woun Employee)

고용인 (go-yong-in = 임직원, Worker, Employee) 매상 (mae-sang Sales, Income)

총수입 (chong-su-ib Total Income , Gross Revenue) 총지출(chong-zi-chul Total Expense)

년간(nyuhn-gan Annual) 세금(se-geum Tax) 번창 (buhn-chang Good Business,)

성공(suhng-gong Success) 복덩방 (bog-duhg-bang Realtor) 집(zib house)

선금(suhn-geum Downpay)구입 (gu-ib Purchase , Buy)

부동산(bu-dong-san Property) 재산 (zae-san Assets, Earned Money)

관리 (gwan-ri Supervise, Management) 관리원 (gwan-ri-wuhn manager)

@ 외출 (woe-chul Going out   )

상점 (sang-zuhm Store = 가게 ga-ge) 서점 (suh-zuhm Book Store   책 가게)

백화점 (baeg-hwa-zuhm, Department Store) 상가 (sang-ga Mall)

음식점 (eum-sig zuhm   Restaurant   = 식당 sig-dang)

공원 (gong-woun Park) 극장(geug-zang Theater) 영화 (young-hwa Movie)

음악감상실(eum-ag-gam-sang-sil Music Listen Place)

미술관 (mi-sul-gwan Art Gallery) 그림 (geu-rim Picture Paint)

박물관(bag-mul-gwan Museum) 조각 (zo-gag sculptures) 예술 (ye-sul Art)

사진 (sa-zin Photo) 고찰 (go-chal Ancient Temple)

고궁 (go-gung Old Palace) 교회 (gyo-hwoe Church) 목사 (mog-sa Minister, Paster)

성당 (suhng-dang Catholic Church)성모 (suhng-mo Holly Mother) 신부 (sin-bu father)

성경 (suhng-gyuhng Bible) 십자가 (sib-za-ga Cross) 천당 (chun-dang Haven)

영생 (yuhng-saeng Eternal life) 죄 (zwae Sin) 지옥 (zi-okg Hell)

다방 (da-bang Tea Room = 카페 ka-pe Cafe = 싸롱(ssa-rong)

여행 (yuh-haeng Trip, Journey ,Travel = 관광 gwan-gwang)

여행사 (yuh-haeng-sa Travel Center)

목적지 (mog-zuhg-zi Destination) 체류 (che-ryu Stay) 단원(dan-woun Member)

안전 (an-zuhn Safe)

@ 장보기=시장보기 (zang-bo-gi = si-zang-bo-gi Shopping)

옷가게 (ots-ga-ge Clothing Store) 한복 (han-bog Korean traditional clothes)

양복 (yang-bog Western Clothes , Suits) 여성복 (yuh-suhng-big Female Clothes)

남성복 (nam-suhng-big Male Clothes) 양장점 (yang-zang-zuhm Female Custume)

양복점 (yang-bog-zuhm Male Suit Store) 맞춤 (maz-chum Costume Design)

아동복 (a-dong-bog Children's Clothes) 숙녀복 (sug-nyuh-bog Lady's Clothes)

신사복 (sin-sa-bog Gentlemen Clothes) 양복 (yang-bog Suit) 치마 (chi-ma Skirt)

바지 (ba-zi Pants) 드레스 (deu-re-seu Dress) 원피스 (woun-pi-seu = Dress)

투피스 (tu-pi-seu Female Suit) 양복 (yang-bog Male Suit) 셔츠(syuh-cheu Shirt)

속옷 (sog-ots Underwear) 속치마 (sog-chi-ma Slip) 반코트 (ban-ko-teu Half Coat)

긴코트 (gin-ko-teu Long Coat) 장갑 (zang-gab Gloves) 모자 (mo-za Hat)

가방 (ga-bang Bag) 핸드백 (haen-deu-baeg Female hand bag, Purse)

수영복 (su-yuhng-bog Swimming suit) 신발가게 (sin-bal Shoes store =구두가게)

문방구 (mun-bang-gu Stationary) 화장품 (hwa-zang-pum Cosmetics)

식료품가게 (sig-ryo-pum-ga-ge Grocery Store)

정육점 (zuhmg-yug-zuhm Meats Store , butcher shop)

생선가게 (saeng-suhn-ga-ge Fish Store) 시장(si-zang Market)

빵가게 (bbang-ga-ge Bakery) 빵 (bbang Bread)과자(Gwa-za Cookie) 케익(ke-ik Cake)

도매시장 (do-mae-si-zang Whole Sale Market)

소매시장 (so-mae-si-zang Retail Market)

@ 운동구점 (un-dong-gu-zuhm Sporting Goods Store)

운동복 (un-dong-bog Sport Uniform) 야구 (ya-gu Baseball) 농구(nong-gu Basketball)

축구 (chug-gu Soccer) 미식축구(mi-sig-chug-gu Football) 미국 (mi-gug America)

구 (gu Ball= 공 gong) 배구 (bae-gu Volleyball) 탁구 (tag-gu Pingpong)

정구 (zuhng-gu Tennis, Soft ball) 아이스케이트 (a-i-seu-ke-i-teu Ice Skate)

수영 (su-yuhng Swimming) 골프 (gil-peu Golf) 하키 (ha-ki Hockey)

체조(che-zo Gymnastics) 달리기(dal-ri-gi Running) 뜀뛰기 ddeuym-ddeu-gi Jump)

높이뛰기 (nop=i-ddwi-gi Highjump) 하키 (ha-ki Huckey) 스키 (seu-ki Ski)

선수 (suhn-su Player) 심판 (sim-pan Judgement)

@ 주문 (zu-mun Order) 가격 (ga-gyuhg Price) 돈(don Money)

지폐 (zi-pye paper money) 동전 (dong-zuhn coin) 화폐 (hwa-pye currency)

금융 (geum-yung circulation of money) 융자 (yung-za finencing)

단기 (dan-gi short term) 장기 (zang-gi long term) 이자 (i-za interest)

잔돈 (zan-don change)   지불 (zi-bul   Pay) 영수증(yuhng-su-zeung Receipt)

주점 (zu-zuhm Bar = 술집) 덤(duhm Tip, Extra) 비데오가게 (bi-de-o ga-ge Video Store

@ 경찰서 (gyuhng-chal-suh Police Office)

법 (bub Legal , Law) 불법(bul-buhb Illegal) 죄 (zwoe, Sin)신고 (sin-go Report)

통고 (tong-go Notice, Notification)   재판소 (zae-pan-so Court) 판사 (pan-sa   Judge)

변호사 (byun-ho-sa   Lawyer, Attorney) 가해자 (ga-hae-za   Offender)

피해자(pi-hae-za Victim, Damager) 증인 (zeung-in Witness)

목격자 (mog-gyuhg-za Who watched)고소 (go-so   Sue, plaintiff)

신고 (sin-go Report) 법정 (buhb-zuhng Court) 변호 (byuhn-ho Defense , Justification)

선서 (suhn-suh Swear) 판정(pan-zuhng Sentence)

수사(su-sa   Investigation= 조사 zo-sa) 무죄 (mu-zwoe Innocence, Not guilty)

유죄(yu-zwoe Guilty), 법위반 (bub-wi-ban Against the Law =져촉 zuh-chog)

공갈 (gong-gal Threat) 사기(sa-gi Fraud) 유괴 (yu-gwoe Kidnapping)

살인 (sal-in   Murder) 협박 (hyub-bag Menace, Intimidation)

음모 (eum-mo Plot)   선고 (suhn-go Sentence) 별금 (buhl-geum Fine)

감옥 (gam-og Jale, Prison) 수감 (su-gam Imprisonment) 죄수 (zwoe-su   Prisoner)

사형 (sa-hyuhng Death Penalty) 석방 (suhg-bang Release, Discharge   )

@ 병원(byuhng-woun Hospital)

개인병원(gae-in-byuhng-woun Private, Doctor Office) 의사 (euh-sa Doctor)

간호원 (gan-ho-woun Nurse) 응급실 (eung-geub-sil Emergency room)

대기실 (dae-gi-sil Waiting Room) 기다리다 (gi-da-ri-da Wait)

이름(i-reum Name= 성명 suhng-myuhng) 부르다 (bu-reu-da Call)

이리로(i-ri-ro To This Way) 오세요(o-se-yo Come)

저리로 (zuh-ri-ro To There) 가세요 (ga-se-yo Go) 몸무게 (mom-mu-ge Weight)

키 (ki Height) 재다 (zae-da Measure for length, 달다 dal-da for weight   )

\# 여기에 (yuh-gi-e At Here) 앉으세요(anz-zeu-se-yo Sit)

혈압 (hyuhl-ab Blood Pressure) 피 (pi Blood)

고혈압 (go-hyul-ub High Blood Pressure) 저혈압 (zuh-hyul-ub Low Blood Pressure)

소변 (so-byuhn Urine) 체온(che-on Body Temperature)통증 (tong-zeung Pain)

검사 (guhm-sa Test)엑스레이 촬영 (eg-seu-re-i chal-yuhng X-Ray)

\# 나이 (na-i Age) 몇살 (myuhts-sal How old) 이세요 (i-se-yo) ?

생년월일 (saeng-nyuhn-woul-il   Birth year ,month and date)

적으세요 (zuhg-eu-se-yo Write down please = 쓰세요 sseu-se-yo)

\# 어디가 (uh-di-ga   Where) 아프세요 (a-peu-se-yo Pain,   Hurting?)

\# 어지러우세요 (uh-zi-ruh-u-se-yo Are you feel dizzy ?)

\# 소화 (so-hwa Digestion) 잘 (zal Well) 되세요(dwoe-se-yo Does ?)

머리 (muh-ri Head) 얼굴(uhl-gul   Face) 목(mog   Neck) 어깨 (uh-ggae   Shoulder)

가슴 (ga-seum   Chest) 배 (bae   Belly) 등(deung Back) 속 (sog Inside Belly)

위 (wi   Stomach) 머리 (muh-ri Head) 이마 (i-ma   Forehead) 눈 (nun Eye)

코 (ko   Nose) 입 (ib   Mouth) 턱 (tuhg Chin) 귀 (gwi Ear) 얼굴 (uhl-gul   Face)

이 (yi   Teeth = 치아 chi-a =잇발 its-bal) 치과(chi-gwa Dentist)

혀 (hyuh Tongue = 혓바닥 huhts-ba-dag) 목 (mog Neck)

목구멍 (mog-gu-muhng Throat) 숨 (sum Breath =호흡 ho-heup)

위장(wi-zang Stomach) 심장(sim-zang Heart) 폐 (pye Lung)

간 (gan Liver) 창자(chng-za Intestine) 신장 (sin-zang Kidney)

맹장 (maeng-zang Appendix) 결장 (gyuhl-zang Colon) 췌장 (cheh-zang Pancreas)

항문 (hang-mun Anal)질 (zil Vergina) 자궁(za-gung Womb) 어깨 (uh-ggae Shoulder)

가슴(ga-seum Chest) 배 (bae Belly) 허리 (huh-ri Waist) 배꼽 (bae-ggob Navel , Belly

button) 성기(suhng-gi Sex organ) 엉덩이(uhng-duhng-i Hip=궁뎅이 gung-deng-i)

넓적다리(nruhlb-zuhg-da-ri Tigh) 무릎(mu-reup Knee) 다리 (da-ri Leg)

발목 (bal-mog Ankle) 발 (bal feet) 발가락 (bal-ga-rag Toe)

손가락(son-ga-rag Finger) 팔 (pal Arm) 팔굼치 (pal-gum-chi Elbow)

손목 (son-mog Wrist) 손 (son Hand) 손톱 (son-tob Nail)

잠 (zam Sleep) 은 (eun s.s) 잘 (zal Well) 주무세요(zu-mu-se-yo Take a sleep)?

무슨(mu-seun What) 음식 (eum-sig Food) 을 (eul objective s)

잡수셨어요 (zab-su-syuhtss-uh-yo Had Eat) ?

청진기 (chuhng-zin-gi Stethoscope) 내진 (nae-zin Dignose = 진찰 zin-chal)

검사 (guhm-sa Test) 피 (pi Blood = 혈액(hyuhl-aeg) 혈구 (hyuhl-gu Blood Cell)

백혈구(baeg-hyuhl-gu White Blood Cell) 적혈구(zuhg-hyuhl-gu Red Blood Cell)

주사 (zu-sa Injection) 약 (yag Medicine) 처방 (chuh-bang Prescription)

복용 (bog-yong Apply,Taking) 사용법 (sa-yong-buhb Directions for Use)

약사 (yag-sa Pharmacist) 약국 (yag-gug Pharmacy)

@ 종합병원 (zong-hab-byuhng-woun Hospital)

응급실 (eung-geub-sil Emergency Room) 영양주사 (yuhng-yang-zu-sa IV injection)

IV is Intravenous Injection 정맥주사 zuhng-maeg-zu-sa = 링겔주사

산소 마스크 (san-so ma-seu-keu Oxygen Mask) 인공호흡 (in-gomg-ho-heub CPR)

정상(zuhng-sang Nomal) 임신(im-sin Pregnant)

임신부 (im-sin-bu Pregnant Woman) 분만 (bun-man Delivery) 아기(a-gi Baby)

산모 (san-mo Mother of new born baby)

산부인과 (san-bu-in-gwa Obstetrics and Gynecology)

내과 (nae-gwa Internal) 외과(woe-gwa External) 수술과 (su-sul-gwa Surgical)

피부 (pi-bu Skin) 피부과 (pi-bu-gwa Dematology) 뼈 (bbyuh Bone)

근육 (geun-yug Muscle) 뇌 (nwoe Brain) 신경 (sin-gyuhng Nerve) 세포 (se-po Cell)

회복 (hwoe-bog Recovery) 완쾌 (wan-kwoe Completley Recovery)

퇴원 (twoe-woun Discharge , Leaving hospital)

산책 (san-cheg Walk to get fresh air and exercise = 걷기 guhd-gi)

소풍 (so-pung Picnic) 등산 (deung-san Climbing) 수영 (su-yuhng Swimming)

춤 (chum Dance) 관강 (gwan-gang Sightseeing) 여행 (yuh-haeng Travel ,Trip)

방문(bang-mun Visit) 친구 (chin-gu Friend) 친척 (chin-chug Relations)

생일파티 (saeng-il-pa-ti Birthday Party) 공휴일 (gong-hyu-il Holiday)

취미(chwi-mi Hobby) 별장 (byuhl-zang Cottage) 조각 (zo-gag Sculpture)

그림 (geu-rim Picture) 소설 (so-suhl Novel) 이야기 (i-ya-gi story) 시 (si Poem)

독서(dog-suh Reading) 음악 (eum-ag Music) 노래 (no-rae Song) 노래부르다 (Sing)

운동 (un-dong Sports) 맨손체조(maen-son-che-zo Body Stretch)

호흡운동(ho-heub-un-dong Breathing Excercise) 일 (il Work)

정신수양 (zuhng-sin-su-yuhng Mental Care) 종교(zong-gyo Religion)

요리 (yo-ri Cook) 담화 (dam-hwa Conversations = 대화 dae-hwa)

취침 (chwi-chim Sleep = 잠 zam) 숙면 (sug-myuhn Good Sleep)

불면 (bul-myuhn No Sleep) 번민 (buhn-min Wory) 평화 (pyuhng-hwa Peace)

@ 교통 (gyo-tong Traffic , Transportation)

길 (gil Way ,Street) 골목길(gol-mog-gil Alley) 도보(do-bo Side way)

차길 (cha-gil Traffic Lane , Street for driving a car) 자전거 (za-zuhn-guh   Bicycle)

오토바이 (o-to-ba-i   Motorcycle) 자가용 (za-ga-yong Own Car) 버스(buh-seu Bus)

택시 (taeg-si Taxi) 주차장(zu-cha-zang Parking Place) 번호(buhn-ho Number)

정거장 (zuhng-guh-zang Station) 좌석 (zwa-suhg Seat) 운전사 (un-zuhn-sa Driver)

차장 (cha-zang Car Guider) 요금 (yo-geum Fee) 승무원 (seung-mu-woun Crew)

종점 (zong-zuhm   Last station) 목적지 (mog-zuhg-zi Destination)

도착 (do-chag Arrive) 내리다 (nae-ri-da Take off , Get off) 전철 (zuhn-chuhl Subway)

호선(h0-suhn Lane Number) 기차 (gi-cha Train) 배 (bae Ship = 함선 ham-suhn)

군함(gun-ham Navy Ship) 항구(hang-gu Harbor , Port)

@ 비행장 (bi-haeng-wkd Airport = 공항 gong-hang   )

비행기 (bi-haeng-gi Airplane) 비행기표(pyo Airplane Ticket)

조종사 (zo-zomg-sa   Pilot) 안내자 (an-nae-za Guider) 탑승자 (tab-seung-za   Boarder)

승무원 (seung-mu-wuon Crew) 여자 (yuh-za Woman) 남자 (nam-za Man)

아이 (a-i Kids) 아이들(a-i-deul Children) 스튜어디스 (sru-tyu-uh-di-seu   Stewardess)

출입구 (chul-ib-gu Gate, Door) 비상구 (bi-sang-gu Emergency Door)

여행가방 (yuh-haeng-ga-bang Suitcase) 이름표 (i-reum-pyo Name Tag)

비행기표 (bi-haeng-gi-pyo Airline Ticket) 표 (pyo Ticket) 검사 (guhm-sa   Check up)

몸조사 (mom-zo-sa   Body Check-Up) 좌석(zwa-suhg Seat) 창믄 (chang-mun Window)

안전벨트 (an-zuhn-bel-teu Seat-Belt Safety belt) 화장실 (hwa-zang-sil Restroom)

담배 (dam-bae   Cigar , Smoke) 금연 (geum-yuhn   No Smoke)

공기주머니 (gong-gi-zu-muh-ni Air Bag) 음료 (eum-ryo Drinks, Beverages)

물 (mul Water) 차 (cha Tea) 커피 (kuh-pi Coffe)

술 (sul liquor = 주류 zu-ryu) 포도주 (po-do-zu Wine) 소다 (so-da   Soda)

팝(pob   Pop) 땅콩 (dang-kong   Peanut) 과자 (gwa-za   Cookie) 사탕 (sa-tang   Candy)

종이 (zong-i Paper) 책 (chaeg   Book) 잡지(zab-zi Magazine)

@ 배 (bae Ship, Boat) 관강선(gwan-gang-suhn Travel Boat, Cruise)

화물선 (hwa-mul-suhn   Business Boat) 부두 (bu-du   Dock)

군함 (gun-ham   Military Boat) 잠수함 (zam-su-ham   Submarine)

@ 우주 (u-zu, Universe, Space)

지구 (zi-gu, Earth) 태양 (tae-yang = 해 hae, Sun) 별 (byuhl, Star = 성 suhng   )

달 (dal, Moon=월 woul Month) 보름달(bo-reum-dal, Full moon)

화성 (hwa-suhng, Mars) 수성 (su-suhng, Mercury)목성 (mog-suhng, Jupiter)

금성 (geum-suhng, Venus) 토성 (to-suhng, Saturn) 은하수 (eun-ha-su, Milky Way)

@ 요일 (yo-yil, = 날 nal , day)

일요일 (yil-yo-yil Sunday)평일(pyuhng-il Weekday) 공휴일 (gong-hyu-yil   Holiday)

월요일 (wuhl-yo-yil Monday) 화요일 (wha-yo-yil, Tuesday)

수요일 (su-yo-yil, Wednsday) 목요일 (mog-yo-yil,   Thursday)

금요일 (geum-yo-yil, Friday) 토요일 (to-yo-yil, Saturday)

오늘 (o-neul Today) 어제 (uh-ze Yesterday) 그저께 (geu-zuh-gge Before yesterday)

내일 (nae-yil Tomorrow) 모래 (mo-rae After tomorrow)

글피 (geul-pi after after tomorrow)

오늘은 무슨 요일 입니까 ? (o-neul-eun mu-seun nal-ibm-ni-gga   What day is today ?)

수요일 입니다. (su-yo-il-ibm-ni-da It is Wednesday)

무슨 (mu-seun What) 언제 (uhn-ze When)

@ 달 (dal, Month)

일월 (yil-woul, January) 이월 (yi-woul, February) 삼월 (sam-woul, March)

사월 (sa-woul, April) 오월 (o-woul, May) 유월 (yu-woul, June) 칠월(chil-woul, July)

팔월 (pal-woul, August) 구월 (gu-woul, September) 시월 (si-woul, October)

십일월 (sib-il-woul November) 십이월 (sib-i-woul, December)

일년에는 몇 달이 있습니까 ? yil-nyuhn-e-neun myuhts dal-yi iss-seub-ni-gga

How many months in a year ?

열두달이 있습니다 yuhl-du-dal-yi yiss-seub-ni-da   There are twelve months.

일년 (yil-nyuhn One year) 에는 (e-neun   At , In a locative suffix)

몇 (myuhts How many) 달 (dal Month, Moon) 이 (yi a s.ujective s.)

있습니까 (yiss-seum-ni-gga Question shape of 있습니다)

까 (gga Questioning suffix)

있습니다 (yits-seum-ni-das Are or Is) 열두(yuhl-du Twelve)

@ 년 (nyuhn, Year) 달력 (dal-ryuhg, Calendar)

단기 (dan-gi Traditinal Korean Calendar , 2333 years older then A.D.)

서기 (suh-gi A.D. ; Anno Domini The Calender Christian Version)

양력 (yang-ryuhg Solar Calendar) 음력 (eum-ryhg, Lunar Calendar)

일월 (yil=woul, January) 이월 (yi-woul, February) 삼월 (sam-woul, March)

사월 (sa-woul, April) 오월 (o-woul, May) 유월 (yu-woul June) 칠월 (chil-woul July)

팔월 (pal-woul August) 구월 (gu-woul September) 시월 (si-woul October)

십일월 (sib-yil-woul November) 십이월 (sib-yi-woul December)

@ 계절 (gye-zuhl Seasons)

봄 (bom, Spring) 여름 (yuh-reum, Summer)

가을 (ga-eul, Autumm) 겨울 (gyh-ul, Winter)

@ 방향 (bang-hang, Direction)

동 (dong, East) 서 (suh, West) 남 (nam, South) 북 (bug, North)

@ 자연 (za-yuhn, Nature)

산 (san, Mountain) 바다 (ba-da, Sea) 대양 (dae-yang, Ocean) 들 (deul, Field)

벌판 (buhl-pan, Plain) 호수 (ho-su, Lake) 강 (gang, River)

시냇물 (si-naets-mul Stream) 물 (mul, Water) 폭포(pog-po Falls)

바람 (ba-ram, Wind = 풍 pung) 동풍 (dong-pung East wind)

서풍 (suh-pung West wind) 남풍 (nam-pung, South wind)

북풍 (bug-pung, North wind) 회오리바람 (hwoe-o-ri-ba-ram Twister)

태풍 (tae-pung, Typhoon) 비(bi, Rain) 번개 (buhn-gae, Lightning)

천둥 (chun-dung, Thunder) 장마 (zang-ma, Heavy rain season) 눈 (nun, Snow)

구름 (gu-reum, Clouds) 무지게 (mu-zi-ge, Rainbow)

무지게는 어디에 있읍니까 ? mu-zi-ge-neun uh-di-e iss-eum-ni-gga

Where is the rainbow ?

하늘에 있읍니다 ha-neul-e iss-eum-ni-da

It is at the sky.

어디 (uh-di where) 하늘 (ha-neul Sky)

@ 감정과 동사 (gam-zuhng-gwa dong-sa Feelings and Verbs)

즐겁다 (zeul-guhb-da Joy) 기쁘다 (gi-bbeu-da Delight) 슬프다 (seul-peu-da Sad)

미안하다(mi-an-ha-da Sorry) 감사하다(gam-sa-ha-da Thank you =고맙다 go-mab-da)

배고프다 (bae-go-peu-da Hungry 배고파 ? = 시장하세요 ? si-zang-ha-se-yo, in polite)

화내다 (hwa-nae-da Angry , Mad = 성내다 suhng-nae-da)아프다 (a-peu-da Hurt ,Sick)

괜찮다 (gaenh-chan-da Fine) 귀찮다(gwi-chan-da Bother) 만사(man-sa Every Matter)

피곤하다 (pi-gon-ha-da Tired) 쉬다 (swi-da Rest)

편안하다 (pyuhn-an-ha-da Comfortable) 졸립다 (zol-rib-da Sleepy) 잠 (zam Sleep)

잔다 (zan-da Sleeping) 꿈 (ggum , Dream , noun shape)

꿈꾸다 (ggum-ggu-da Dream , verb shape) 기분 (gi-bun Feeling)

좋다 (zoth-da Good , Nice) 웃다 (uts-da Laugh) 울다 (ul-da Cry)

살것같다 (sal-guhs-gat-da Feel Alive) 죽겠다 (zug-getss-da Feel Die)

@ 예쁘다 (ye-bbeu-da Pretty) 아름답다(a-reum-dab-da Beautiful)

우아하다 (u-a-ha-da Graceful) 고상하다 (go-sang-ha-da Elegant)

행복하다 (haeng-bog-a-da Happy) 상냥하다 (sang-nyang-ha-da Delight and Friendly)

진심이다 (zin-sim-i-da Sincerely) 귀엽다(gwi-yuhb-da Cute)

잘생겼다(zal-saeng-gyutss-da Handsome) 친절하다 (chin-zuhl-ha-da Kind)

예의바르다 (ye-euy-ba-reu-da Courteous) 근사하다 (geun-sa-ha-da Looks Perfect)

끝내준다 (ggeut-nae-zun-da That Set , Hot) 삼삼하다 (sam-sam-ha-da Looks Nice)

매력 (mae-ryuhg Attraction) 매력적 (mae-ryuhg-zuhg Attractive)

쌕씨 (ssaeg-ssl Sexy = 성적매력 suhng-zuhg-mae-ryuhg Sexual Attractions)

멋았다 (muhts-itss-da Cool, Stylish , Fashionable = 멋지다 muhts-zi-da)

미끈하다 (mi-ggeun-ha-da Sleek) 깨끗하다 (ggae-ggeuts-ha-da Clean)

밝다 (barg-da Bright = 환하다 hwan-ha-da) 어둡다 (uh-dub-da Dark)

희미하다 (heui-mi-ha-da Dimness, not clear)

말하다 (mal-ha-da Talk = 이야기하다 i-ya-gi-ha-da) 대화하다 (dae-hwa-ha-da Conversation)

정답다 (zuhng-dab-da Friendly) 다정하다 (da-zuhng-ha-da Affectionate)

기다 (gi-da Crawl) 가다 (ga-da Go = 간다 gan-da) 오다 (o-da Come = 온다 on-da)

걷다 (guhd-da Walk) 뛰다 (ddwi-da Run) 뜀뛰다 (ddwim-ddwi-da Jump)

날다 (nal-da Fly)뒹군다(dwing-gun-da Roll Over)스다 (seu-da Stand uP= 슨다 seun-da)

멈추다 (muhm-chu-da Stop) 맛 (mats Taste) 맛있다(mats-itss-da Delicious ,Tasty)

짜다 (zza-da Salty) 달다 (dal-da Sweet) 시다 (si-da Sour, Acid)

쓰다 (sseu-da Bitter, Write, Put on, Use) 춤추다 (chum-chu-da Dance)

노래하다 (no-rae-ha-da Sing)일하다 (il-ha-da Work) 논다 (non-da Not Work . No Job)

작난하다 (zag-nan-ha-da Play) 게으르다 (ge-eu-reu-da Lazy)

부지런하다 (bu-zi-ruhn-ha-da Diligent) 열심 (yuhl-sim Enthusiasm)

잘산다 (zal-san-da Living Well = 부자 bu-za Rich)

못산다 (mots-san-da Poor = 가난하다 ga-nan-ha-da)

보통 (bo-tong Medium Class = 중간 zung-gan)

고급 (go-geub High Class) 유행 (yu-haeng Trend) 첨단 (chum-dan Van Guard)

고풍 (go-pung Classic) 현대 (hyuhn-dae Modern)

@ 덥다 (duhb-da Warm) 뜨겁다 (ddeu-guhb-da Hot)

차다 (cha-da Cold = 차겁다 cha-guhb-da = 춥다 chub-da)

감기 (gam-gi Cold) 감기걸렸다 (gam-gi-guhl-ryuhtss-da Catch Cold)

병 (byuhng Sickness , Disease) 약 (yag Medicine) 복용 (bog-yong Take)

나았다 (na-atss-da Get Well) 회복 (hwoe-bog Recover) 완전 (wan-zuhn Complete)

잘 (zal Well) 한다 (han-da Doing) 좋다 (zoth-da Good) 나쁘다 (na-bbeu-da Bad)

어질렀다 (uh-zil-ruhtss-da Mashed Up) 더럽다 (duh-ruhb-da Dirty)

뒤죽박죽 (dwi-zug-bakg-zug Mashed Up = 엉망진창 uhng-mang-zin-chang)

정돈하다 (zuhng-don-ha-da   Organized , Cleaned = 치웠다 chi-woutss-da)

깨끗하다 (ggae-ggeuts-ha-da Clean) 보기좋다(bo-gi-zoth-da Looks Good)

시작하다 (si-zag-ha-da Start) 끝마치다(ggeut-ma-chi-da Finish)

@ 집구조 (Zib-gu-zo, House Constructions)

일층집(yil-cheung-zib, One story house =단층집 (dan-cheung zib)

이층집 (yi-cheung-zib,   Two story house)이층 (i-cheung Upstair)

안방 (an-bang, Master room , 방 means Room) 마루(ma-ru, Wooden floor)

대청 (dae-chuhng, big 마루) 건너방 (guhn-nuh-bang, Next room of floor)

온돌방 (on-dol-bang, Stoned floor room ; 온 means Warm 돌 means Stone)

아랫목(ah-rawts-mog, Near fire place warm spots in Ondol room)

운목 (wun-mog = 윗목 wits-mog, Further spots from 아랫목)

공부방 (gong-bu-bang Study room) 객실 (gaeg-sil= 손님방 son-nim-bang= Guest room)

다락 (da-rag, Small room under the roof)

부엌 (bu-uhk   kitchen) 창고 (chang-go, Store house) 차고 (cha-go, Car garage)

\# 목욕실 (mog-yog-sil, Shower room with bath tub)

화장실(hwa-zang-sil, Restroom) 변소 (buhn-so, Toilet)

, 뜰 (ddeul,= 정원 zuhng-woun, Garden) 밭 (bat Plant garden)

꽃밭 (ggot-bat Flower garden) 정자 (zuhng-za, Summer house in gasrden)

지붕 (zi-bung, Roof) 문 (mun, Door) 창문(chang-mun, Window)

대문 (dae-mun, Gate) 문패 (mun-pae, Master's name pad)

자가용 (za-ga-yong, Owned car) 차 (cha, Car)

가정부 (ga-zuhng-bu, Housemaid = 파출부 pa-chul-bu)

@ 가구 (ga-gu Furniture)

침대 (chim-dae, Bed) 옷장(ots-zang Wardrobe) 문갑 (mun-gab, Chest)

경대 (gyuhng-dae, Dresser) 화장대 (hwa-zang-dae, Make up dresser , Powder dresser)

등잔(deung-zan, Lamp) 이불장 (yi-bul-zang Comforters wardrobe)

이불 (yi-bul, Comforter) 이불보 (yi-bul-bo, Comforter's cover)

요 (yo,   Mattress = 요대기 , yo-dae-gi) 비게 (bi-ge, Pillow)

장판 (zang-pan,   Floor mat) 의자 (euy-za Chair=걸상 guhl-sang),

안락의자 (an-rag-euy-za, Couch, Sofa = 소파) 탁자 (tag-za Table, Desk)

식탁 (sig-tag, Dining table) 책상 (chaeg-sang, Study desk)

책꽂이 (chaeg-ggotz-i, Bookshelf) 옷걸이 (ots-guhl-i Hanger)

벽장 (byuhg-zang, Closet) 화병 (hwa-byuhng, Flower vase = 꽃병 (ggotch-byuhng)

꽃 is flower 병 is vase, bottle

@ 부엌살림 (bu-uhk-sal-rim, Kitchen funiture and tools)

찬장 (chan-zang, China cabinet =그릇장 geu-reuts-zang)

밥상(bab-sang, Portable dining table)밥그릇 (bab-geu-reuts, Rice bowl = 공기 gung-gi)

반찬그릇 (ban-chan-geu-reuts, Side dish bowl) 접시 (zuhb-si, Dish , plate)

대접 (dae-zuhb Big-dish) 사발 (sa-bal, Porcelain bowl)

주발 (zu-bal, Bress bowl, ceramic, stainless iron or plastic bowls)

양재기(yang-zae-gi, Aluminum bowl) 쟁반(zaeng-ban, Tray ,Server)

은쟁반 (eun-zaeng-ban, Silver tray) 수저 (su-zuh, Spoon and chopsticks)

숟가락 (sutd-ga-rag Spoon) 젓가락 (zuhts-ga-rag Chopsticks)

도마 (do-ma, Chopping board) 칼 (kal, Knife) 절구 (zuhl-gu, Motar)

쇠절구 (swoe-zuhl-gu, Iron motar) 나무절구 (na-mu-zuhl-gu, Wooden motar)

방망이 (bang-mang-i, Mash bat) 항아리 (hang-a-fi, Jar, Pot= 독 dog)

된장독(dwoen-zang-dog, Soybean paste jar) 간장독 (gan-zang-dog, Soy sauce jar)

고추장독 (go-chu-zang-dog, Hot paste jar) 쌀독(ssal-dog, Rice jar)

김치독 (gim-chi-dog, kimchi jar) 깨소금단지(ggae-so-geum-dan-zi, Sesame and salt pot)

바가지 (ba-ga-zi,Dipper) 바구니 (ba-gu-ni, Bamboo basket)

화로 (hwa-ro Portable Oven) 연탄불 (yuhn-tan-bul Charcoal cake Oven)

풍로(pung-ro,Portable charcoal grill) 곤로 (gon-ro, Electric grill) 오븐 (o-beun Oven)

석쇠 (suhg-swoe, Fish baking iron plate) 불 (bul, Fire = 화 hwa)

불고기구이판 (bul-go-gi-gu-i-pan Barbeque grill plate)

전기밥솥 (zuhn-gi-bab-sot, Electric rice cooker)

연탄아궁이 (yuhn-tan-a-gung-i, Chacoal heater tunnel for floor)

개수대 (gae-su-dae, Sink) 수도 (su-do, Pipe water)

설겆이통 (suhl-guhz-i-tong, Dish wash jar or container) 솔(sol Buush)

고무장갑 (go-mu-zang-gab, Rubber gloves) 쑤세미 (ssu-se-mi Scrapper)

@ 세탁 (se- tag, Laundry = 빨래 bbal-rae) 세탁소 (se-tag-so Dry Cleaner)

세탁소는 어디에 있읍니까 ?   se-tag-so-neun uh-di-e iss-eum-ni-gga

Where is the Dry Cleaner ?

저기 식당 옆에 있읍니다   zuh-gi sig-dang uhp-e iss-eum-ni-da

There is the next of restaurant at)

저기 (zuh-gi There,) 식당 (sig-dang Resturant) 옆 (yup Next)

세탁기계 (se-tag-gi-gye, Washer) 비누 (binu Soap)

세탁비누 (se-tag-bi-nu, Detergent) 물비누 (mul-bi-su Liquid soap)

가루비누(ga-ru-bi-nu   Powder detergent)

표백제 (pyo-baeg-ze, Bleaching soap = 양잿물 yang-zaets-mul,)

빨래판 (bbal-rae-pan Washing board) 빨래줄 (bbal-rae-zul, Dryline)

빨래걸이 (bbal-rae-guhl-i, Drying hanger) 세면대 (se-myuhn-dae, Wash face sink)

세수비누 (se-su-bi-nu   Wash face soap) 수건 (su-guhn, Towel)

세숫대야 (se-suts-dae-ya, Wash face basin = 대야)

치약 (chi-yag   Toothpaste) 칫솔 (chits-sol Toothbrush)

구취제거약 (gu-chi-ze-guh-yag Mouth wash)

@ 음식(eum-sig, Food, ready to eat)

밥 (bab, Cooked rice , 쌀 ssal, Raw rice) 흰밥 (heuin-bab, White rice,= 백반 baeg-ban)

콩밥 (kong-bab, Bean rice) 보리밥 (bo-ri-bab, Barley rice)

잡곡밥 (zab-gog-bab Mixed grains rice)   콩나물밥 (kong-na-mul-bab, Bean sprout rice)

김밥 (gim-bab Seaweed rolled with rice, meats and vegetables)

볶음밥 (bog-eun-bab, Stir fry with cooked rice and any favorites)

비빔밥 (bi-bim-bab, Mixed 밥 and any favorites with hot paste)

@ 김치 (gim-chi , known as Kimchi)

(Pickled cabbages with salt and set a half day then wash them ,drain waters

and mixed up with garlics, green onions, gingers, and red hot pepper powder)

p.s. adding salted anchovy (멸치젓) or shrimp (새우젓) is uptional.

배추김치(bae-chu-gimchi, Cabbage gimchi or kimchi)

무우김치 (mu-u-gim-chi, Sliced radish gimchi = 무김치)

열무김치 (yuhl-mu-gimchi, Turnip and it's roots gimchi)

총각김치 (chong-gag-gim-chi Unsliced whole radish gimchi,

총각   chong-gag means Bachelor)

깍두기 (ggag-ddu-gi   Cube shaped radish gimchi)

오이김치 (o-i-gim-chi, Cucumber gimchi)

다꽝 (da-ggwang   Picled yellow sweet radish, japanise style)

@ 국 (gug, Soup)

미역국 (mi-yuhg-gug, Sea weed soup)

된장국 (dwoen-zang-gug, Soy bean paste soup with any favorites   )

콩나물국 (kong-na-mul-gug Bean sprout soup)   소고기국 (so-go-gi-gug, Beef soup)

떡만두국 (dduhg-man-du-gug Sliced rice cakes and dumpling soup)

시금치국(si-geum-chi-gug Spinach soup),해장국(hae-zang-gug Hangover relief soup)

@ 김치찌게 (gimchi-zzi-ge Kimchi stew)

두부찌게 (du-bu-zzi-ge, Tufu stew) 된장찌게,(dweon-zang-zzi-ge, Soy bean paste stew)

장조림 (zang-zo-rim, Beef roast with soy sauce, garic, and sugar)

갈비탕 (gal-bi-tang, Seasoned Beef ribs slow cooked stew)

설농탕 (suhl-nong-tang, Beef meats and bones slow cooked stew)

대구탕 (dae-gu-tang, Cod fish stew)

도가니탕 (do-ga-ni-tang Beef intestines and other good things soup)

탕수육 (tang-su-yug Sweet and sour chicken)

육계장 (yug-gye-zang Hot pepper chicken, cabages, noodle soup)

@ 불고기 (bul-go-gi,   Barbeque meat 불 bul means fire)

소고기 (so-go-gi, Beef ; 소 means the Cow   고기 means the meat)

불고기 (bul-go-gi,   Barbeque beef in usual)

돼지불고기(dwoe-zi-bul-go-gi, Pork barbeque)

불갈비 (bul-gal-bi, Barbequed short ribs) 갈비졸임(gal-bi-zol-im , cook to steam out of seasoned ribs)

갈비찜 (gal-bi-zzim Steam seasoned ribs)

족발 (zog-bal, Pork feet,= 돼지족발 dwoe-zi   Pig's feet)

@ 잡채 (zab-chae,   Mixed vegetables, beef, and clear noodles)

비빔국수 (bi-bim-gug-su Mixed noodle with favorite ingridients)

짜장면 (zza-zang-myuhn Mixed noodles, pork, onions, carrots with black soy paste like the spagetti)

냉면 (naeng-myuhn, Cold season noodles)

함흥냉면 (ham-heung-naeng-myuhn Cold noodles with hong-uh)

홍어회 (hong-uh-hwoe,   Hot red pepper seasoned raw skate fish)

@ 생선 (saeng-suhn, Fish) and 해산물 (hae-san-mul Sea Food)

회 (hwoe, Sliced raw fish = 생선회 = Sasimi)

생선조림 (saeng-suhn-zo-rim, Steamed seasoned fishes)

생선부침 (saeng-suhn-bu-chim, Fish cakes) 생선찜   saeng-suhn-zzim, Steamed fish)

생선구이 (saeng-suhn-gu-i Baked fish) 해삼 (hae-sam, Sea cucumber)

멍게 (muhng-ge, Sea squirt) 굴 (gul, Oyster) 굴젓 (gul-zuhtz, Salted oysters, pickled)

어리굴젓 (uh-ri-gul-zuhtz =굴젓) 알젓 (al-zuhtz, Pickled fish eggs)

게찌게 (ge-zzi-ge Crabs stew) 참게 (cham-ge Small crab)

게장 (ge-zang   Pickled crabs with soy souce) 조개탕 (zo-gae-tang   Clam stew)

멸치볶음 (myuhl-chi-bog-eum, Stirred seasoned anchovy)

새우 (sae-u Shrimp) 새우젓 (sae-u-zuhs salted shrimps)

오징어볶음 (o-zing-uh-bogg-eum, Stirred seasoned squirts)

오징어젓 (o-zing-uh-zuhtz, Pickled squirts)

@ 고사리무침 (go-sa-ri-mu-chim, Seasoned ferns)

시금치 무침 (si-geum-chi mu-chim   seasoned spinach)

도라지무침 (do-ra-zi-mu-chim, Seasoned bell flower roots) 오이무침 (o-i mu-chim seasoned cucumber)

콩나물무침 (kong-na-mul mu-chim seasoned bean spurots)

미역무침 (mi-yuhg mu-chim seasoned sea weeds) 콩자반(kong-za-ban, Baked beans)

장조림 (zang-zo-rim Bioled beef with soy sauce and sugar)

김 (gim,   Dried and shaped sea weeds usually black color and rectangle shape)

파래 (pa-rae, Green sea weed) 미역 (mi-yuhg, Big leaf sea weed)

가지무침 (ga-zi-mu-chim, Sliced and cook or steam the seasoned egg plants)

녹두부침 (nog-du-bu-chim, Green bean pan cakes)

무침 (mu-chim means all ingredients mixed up together for season them with cooked or raw to serve)

부침 (bu-chim means bake foods in the pan with oils like pan cake , for any vegetables, fishes)

@ 두부 (du-bu, Soy bean cheese , Tufu)

두부부침 (du-bu-bu-chim, Tufu pan cakes) 두부찌게 (du-bu-zzi-ge, 두부 stew)

김치두부찌게 (gim-chi-du-bu-zzi-ge Gimchi and tufu stew)

감자부침 (gam-za-bu-chim, Potato pancakes) 고구마 (go-gu-ma, Sweet potato)

감자 (gam-za Potato) 군고구마 (gun-go-gu-ma, Baked sweet potato)

@ 깨 (ggae, Sesame seed = 참깨 cham-ggae) 들깨 (deul-ggae Wild sesame)

소금 (so-geum Salt) 후추 (hu-chu Black pepper) 깨소금 (ggae-so-geum Mixed sesame seed and salt)

참기름 (cham-gi-reum Sesame oil) 깻잎 (ggaets-ip Sesame leaf)

잎(ip ,Leaf = 잎사귀 ip-sa-gwi)깻잎조림,(ggaets-ip-zo-rim Baked seasonings 깻잎)

깻잎무침 (ggaets-ip-mu-chim Seasoned raw 깻잎),

깻잎쌈 (ggaets-up-ssam, Wrapping, with 깻잎 for any food , 쌈 ssam means wrapping)

상추쌈 (san-chu-ssam, Wrapping with lettuce for rice or any other food)

@ 당신은 무슨 음식을 주문 하시겠습니까 ?

dang-sin-eun mu-seun eum-sig-eul zu-mun ha-si-gess-seum-ni-gga

Which food would you like to order ?

\# 저는 비빔밥을 주문하겠습니다. zuh-neun bi-bim-bab-eul zu-mun-ha-gess-seum-nida.

I would like to order the Bibimbab please.

\# 맛이 어떻습니까 ? mas-i uh-dduhh-seum-ni-gga ?   How is the taste ?

\# 아주 맛있습니다   a-zu-mas-iss- seub-ni-da It is very dilicious.

\# 감사합니다   gam-sa-hab-ni-da Thank you.

당신 (dang-sin You) 은 (eun s.s.) 무슨 (mu-seun Which,= 어떤 uh-dduhn)

음식 (eum-sig Food)을(eul, a object suffix) 주문 (zu-mun   Order) 하시겠습니까 (ha-si-gets-seum-ni-gga Would like to)

나는 (na-neun I) 비빔밥 (bi-bim-bab Bibimbab) 맛 (mats Taste)

이 (yi a subjective suffix) 어떻읍니까 (uh-dduhts-eum-ni-gga How is)

아주 (a-zu Very) 맛있읍니다 (mats-itss-eum-nida,= 맛있다 Delicious)

감사합니다 (gam-sa-ham-ni-da Thank you)

@ 고추 (go-chu, Pepper) 풋고추 (put-go-chu , Unriped green pepper, not hot pepper)

매운고추(mae-wun-go-chu Riped hot pepper)빨강고추 (bbal-gang-go-chu, Red pepper)

고추가루 (go-chu-ga-ru, Pepper powder , red and hot)

고추지 (go-chu-zi Pickled pepper)고추장 (go-chu-zang   Hot pepper pastes)

고추장볶음(go-chu-zang-bog-eum Baked 고추장 with meats)

@ 기타 (gi-ta , The others, 등등 deung-deung)

바섯볶음 (buh-suhts-bog-eum , Stir fried mushrooms)

청포묵 (chuhng-po-mug , Green bean jello ; jello means 묵)

도토리묵 (do-to-ri-mug   Acorn jello)뻔데기 (bbuhn-de-gi Fried silk worms)

과자 (gwa-za Cookies) 전병 (zuhn-byuhng , fried cakes)

식혜 (sig-hye , Sour taste food that made with certain grains and fishes.)

감주 (gam-zu Rice soda , Sweet drinls from rices) 떡 (dduhg Cakes)

흰떡 (heuyn-dduhg White regula rice cakes = 백설기 baeg-suhl-gi)

찰떡 (chal-dduhg Sweet Rice cakes = 인절미 in-zuhl-mi)

무지게떡 (mu-zi-ge-dduhg Rainbow cake that has different colors each layers)

시루떡 (si-ru-dduhg The cakes made by 시루 that jar has holes in bottom for get steams from under boiler

콩떡 (kong-dduhg Bean Cakes) 팥떡 (pat-dduhg Red Bean Cake)

잡곡떡 (zab-gog-dduhg All grains mixed cake)

@ 야채 (ya-chae , Vegetables)

배추 (bae-chu , Cabbage) 무우 (mu-wu , Radish) 상추 (sang-chu Lettuce)

고추 (go-chu , Pepper) 시금치 (si-geum-chi Spinach) 당근 (dang-geun Carrot)

파 (pa , Green onion) 양파 (yang-pa Onion)미나리 (mi-na-ri Dropwort)

쑥갓 (ssug-gats Crown daisy) 오이 (o-i Cucumber) 호박(ho-bag , Zucchini)

들깨 (deul-ggae Sesame) 가지 (ga-zi Egg plant) 버섯 (buh-suhts Mushroom)

부추 (bu-chu Leek)시금치(si-geum-chi Spinach)

@ 과일 (gwa-il Fruit)

사과 (sa-gwa Apple) 배 (bae Pear) 자두 (za-du,Plum) 복숭아 (bog-sung-a Peach)

귤(gyul Orange)포도 (po-do Grapes) 감 (gam Persimmon)

딸기 (ddal-gi Strawberries) 수박 (su bag Watermelon)참외 (cham-woe, Melon)

뺏지 (bbuhts-zi Cherry) 바나나 (ba-ba-na Banana) 대추 (dae-chu Dates)

@ 열매 (yuhl-mae Nuts)

밤 (bam, Chestnuts) 잣 (zatz Pine tree nuts) 호두 (ho-du Walnuts)

땅콩 (ddang-kong Peanuts)

@ 인삼 (yin-sam Ginseng)

인삼은 다년생 뿌리이다   yin-sam-eun da-nyuhn-saeng bbu-ri-i-da

The ginseng is the multi years grown roots.

인삼은 한국의 특산물이고 yin-sam-eun han-gug-euy teug-san-mul-i-go

The ginseng is a special products of Korea and

약효가 있는 식물 이다 yag-hyo-ga itss-neun sig-mul i-da

The plant has the efficiency of medicine.

인삼의 종류는   yin-sam-euy zong-ryu-neun

The kinds of the ginsengs are

수삼과 건삼이 있고   su-sam-gwa guhn-sam i itss-go

the water ginseng and the dried ginseng

인삼차로 널리 쓰인다 yin-sam-cha-ro nuhl-ri sseu-in-da

has been used with the ginseng tea widely

인삼(ginsang) 은(s.s) 다년생 (multy years) 뿌리 (root)이다 (is)

특산물 (special product) 이고 (and)약 (medicine) 효(efficiency = 효과 hyo-gwa)

가(s.s)식물(plant) 종류 (kind. class) 수삼 (water ginseng)건삼 (dried ginseng)

인삼차(ginseng tea) 널리(widely) 쓰인다 (has been used)

@ 한국의 풍속 놀이   han-gug-euy pung-sog nol-i   Korea's traditional Games

그네 (geu-ne Swing) 윷놀이 (yutch-nol-i Four Sticks Play)

탈춤놀이 (tal-chum-nol-i Mask Dance Play)

널뛰기 (nuhl-ddwi-gi Jump on the Wood Board like jumping Seesaw)

북치기 (bug-chi-gi Drum play)

줄다리기 (zul-da-ri-gi Pulling Rope) 씨름(ssi-reum Wrestling)

강강수월래(gang-gang-su-woul-rae The group dance with hand to hand on circle)

This paint by my mom " 남대문 ".

I would like to honor my mom who would taught and loved me.

No.19 my dreams are where I am (나의 꿈은 내가 있는 곳에)

나는 꿈을 꿉니다 I was dreaming .

na-neun ggum-eul ggum-ni-da

내가 어렸을 때도   when I was young

nae-ga uh-ryuhts-eul ddae-do

그리고 지금처럼 어른이 되었어도   and even as I am grown up.

geu-ri-go zi-geum-chuh-ruhm uh-reun-i dwoe-uhtss-uh-do

나는 꿈을 꿉니다 I am dreaming .

na-neun ggum-eul ggum-ni-da

나의 꿈은 색갈이 있습니다 My dreams have colors,

na-euh ggum-eun saeg-gal-i yits-eum-ni-da

어떤 꿈은 이루워집니다   some of them come true

uh-dduhn ggum-eun yi-ru-woe-zimb-ni-da

나의 꿈은 내가 있는 곳에 My dreams are where I am.

na-eu ggum-eun nae-ga yits-neun gots-e

시편 , Poem by The Author Moonhee L. Cho 조(이) 문희

P.S.   I would   wish all your dreams will come true, and see you on YouTube.

저는 여러분들의 모든 꿈이 이루어 지시기를 바라며

유튭에서 만납시다

Thank you 감사합니다

www.ingramcontent.com/pod-product-compliance
Lightning Source LLC
Chambersburg PA
CBHW041550220426
43666CB00002B/28